AN OCEAN DIVIDES ME

Eleanor McArevey Price

First published in Australia by Eleanor McArevey Price

This edition published 2025
Copyright © Eleanor McArevey Price 2025

Typesetting and e-book design: Amit Dey (amitdey2528@gmail.com)
Cover design: Talia Lev (tallevdesign.com)

The right of Eleanor McArevey Price to be identified as Author of the
Work has been asserted in accordance with the Copyright, Designs and
Patents Act 1988.

ISBN number: 978-1-923298-23-1 (paperback)

A catalogue record for this
book is available from the
National Library of Australia

DEDICATION

To my son-in-law, Cador Pricejones,
who helped me bring this story to completion.

ACKNOWLEDGEMENTS

My thanks go to my daughter Margaret, my grand-daughter Esmay Pricejones, other members of my family in Ireland and England, Dr June Davison, and my writing group for their help and advice.

CONTENTS

PREFACE

I grew up in Dublin during World War II. My mother's family, the O'Keefes, came from Wexford; my father's family, the McAreveys, came from Newry, in Northern Ireland. My family were known as Papists, or 'Castle Catholics' and had held their land since as far back as the Cromwellian Settlement (1649–1653). My grandfather, William J. O'Keefe, was a maltster, a professional who prepares malt from grain. My mother was one of William and his wife Lilly's eight children. My father went to Clongowes Wood College, a private Jesuit school in Kildare and had a medical degree from University College Dublin.

My three younger sisters, Ann, Mary Rose and Esmay, were part of the household, as was Aunty Daisy, my mother's eldest sister.

❧❦❧

Ireland didn't become a republic until 1928. There were no local industries, or government subsidies for the poor-performing national schools. Ireland had some of the worst slums in Europe; however, we were privileged children, though unaware of it at the time.

My sisters and I went to private schools, and I was a good student, ambitious and conscious of the political divide in the Republic. Since many of my fellow students had strong political alliances, we never discussed politics after the revolt of 1916. My family was politically conservative, supporting the Fine Gael party, and would have voted for Parnell, the Treaty, and Michael Collins.

I attended University College Dublin and received a Degree in Architecture. After my father died, I worked briefly in London and followed my older cousins to Southern Rhodesia, where I got a good job with two young English architects in Salisbury, the capital city. When Rhodesia started the transition to becoming Zimbabwe, I returned to Europe.

Though I had no plans to go to the United States at the time, I received an invitation to visit California, which I accepted. I ended up moving to San Francisco and became part of a group of young professionals from Ireland, England, and other places in Europe in search of sunshine, good jobs, and a new perspective.

I also contacted an old friend of my mother from Wexford, Dr Clare Malone, who had gone to California in the 1920s. She told me something I'll never forget.

"You may work hard, get married and have children, but you will never be truly American. In spite of my success in this country, my heart will always be in Wexford."

❧•❧

Time passed, and life on San Francisco's Telegraph Hill was losing its appeal when the offer of a rent-controlled apartment on the Upper East side of New York City

(NYC) clinched the deal. I quickly settled into the New York lifestyle, learnt to ride the subway, got an interesting job, and met Don Price, a lawyer originally from Minnesota.

We fell in love and got married. In place of a formal wedding, we took an extended wedding trip to Europe and Minnesota.

Back in the USA, we bought a fixer-up house in Montclair, a New Jersey suburb, and had two children, Margaret and John.

❧·❧

With so many architect-designed houses in Montclair, I presented my idea of documenting all the houses to the Planning Board and earned a Master's Degree in Historic Preservation at Columbia University.

The children grew up; John attended the University of Pennsylvania, and Margaret went to Bowdoin College in Maine. Don had open-heart surgery in NYC and then decided that he wanted to retire to the south.

We bought our dream house on a two-acre plot in Wilmington, North Carolina – two of the happiest years of my life.

Margaret married Cador Jones. Don's health declined, and he eventually died. When Margaret encouraged me to move closer to her, I sold my house and drove north.

With Cador's help I found a lovely apartment with a front porch and a honeysuckle hedge in Cambridge. I collected Essie and Powell from nursery school, and they often stayed overnight. It brought back memories and joys of raising John and Margaret.

I developed a life of my own, was accepted at the Harvard Institute of Learning in Retirement and made new friends. After several years, living alone was too difficult for me. Consequently, Cador and Margaret gave notice to their first floor tenants and Cador refurbished the apartment. Esmay and Powell helped with the construction. Having lived in a variety of inappropriate apartments with landlords who never fixed anything, I was happy to move into this delightful space with two bedrooms, a large living and dining room, a study, state-of-the-art bathroom, and kitchen.

Now, years later, I'm still here and grateful to those who made it possible.

ANOTHER TIME, ANOTHER PLACE

April 30, 1933

Our family lived in a four-story house on Baggot Street in Dublin. The narrow façade lacked the elegance of the nearby houses, but to us it was home – a place of laughter and fun, with more than enough room for my parents, Aunty Daisy, and three little girls.

My father, a doctor, had his consulting rooms on a return at the back of the house. As children, we were relegated to the fourth floor, where we ate most of our meals under the supervision of a nanny. Running up and down the stairs during my father's office hours was strictly forbidden, though we sometimes broke the rules, sliding down the banisters to snoop at the patients.

The pocket-sized garden with its single lilac bush was a dark, gloomy place between our house and the mews where the Duff family lived. Mummy sent over food, our cast-off clothing, and blankets. I remember Christy, the eldest Duff daughter – skinny and sad-faced, never without a runny nose. They never paid rent.

I loved the street noises – the horse-drawn van that delivered milk in the early morning, the rattle of coal delivered via a scuttle through a chute in the pavement, and the shrill voices of young boys selling newspapers. The sound of the double-decker tram as it click-clacked down the centre of the street to Ballsbridge, lulled us to sleep.

The house was close to the corner of the street and faced a newsagent's shop that sold everything from sweets to comic books. My mother often complained about the noise from the pub and the men that loitered outside the turf accountant's shop next door.

"What's a turf accountant?" I asked her one day.

"It's a place where people make bets on horses. Like a sweepstake, only the odds are better. It's not a place for little girls."

❧•❧

I recall the day of my sixth birthday. I wore a white dress with frills and puffy sleeves, similar to one often worn by Shirley Temple.

I'd hoped my father would come to the party, but he never did. Looking back now, the only birthday party of mine he ever attended was my 21st, and that was in a hotel. My sister Ann, friends Tiernan and Eunice from the Montessori School, my cousin Derry, and Aunty Daisy sat at the long dining room table, a pyramid of paper crackers in place as the centrepiece. Balloons hung from the glass chandelier, and the room smelt of roses and apple juice. Since we normally ate in the nursery, this was a special treat.

At first, the children were on their best behaviour. Then Tiernan, who was not as shy as he looked, spilt lemonade on Eunice's dress and she burst into tears. I deliberately popped a balloon, frightening my sister Ann, who hid under the table. My cousin Derry, who was trying to talk and eat at the same time, ended up spitting food in all directions. We pulled crackers and popped balloons, causing havoc until the noise became deafening.

"Now children, all this must stop," said Aunty Daisy, in a stern voice. "When you are all finished, you will wash your hands and go upstairs to play in the living room."

And that's exactly what we did.

Aunty Daisy tried to corral us into playing games, without much success. We played hide-and-go-seek and hunt the slipper, chasing each other around the furniture.

When I suggested she put on the latest Shirley Temple record, there was a round of applause and soon we were dancing to the strains of *Animal Crackers in my Soup*.

But it wasn't long before Mummy came upstairs to tell us that the children's parents had arrived. It was time for them to go home.

❧·❧

Daisy had been part of our household for as long as I could remember. Taller than Mummy, she had a pale complexion, marcel-waved hair and a fondness for cardigan suits, which she wore offset with pearls or amber beads. She had strong views on everything, but never offered opinions on household matters, which were my mother's domain.

Though she had a car and went to work, she was always around in the evenings and was there to help us with our homework as we grew older.

❖

My parents took care to shelter us from the poverty and unhealthy conditions in our city, but sometimes they did allude to the truth.

"We have finally got enough money to buy the shoes," said my father one day, referring to the Belvedere Newsboys Club that collected money to provide shoes for the young newspaper boys.

"It's about time," Aunty Daisy replied. "We also need to do something about public health. The flower seller outside my shop coughs all the time. Is there anything I can get for her? She's probably riddled with TB".

My father explained there were too few clinics, too many sick people and not enough doctors.

❖

In keeping with the times, our household was formal. My mother, though loving and kind, handed over the grubby realities of child-raising to a variety of nurses who came and went over the years. They were either genteel women who were down on their luck or raw country girls in search of a better life. They took us for walks, washed our dirty faces, and fed us in the third-floor nursery.

My favourite was Madge Greegan, a rosy-faced country girl from County Wicklow, who was a great storyteller. She eventually left us to marry a local police-man. Another, Lucy Duffy, was absent minded and pious.

However, we never felt neglected. Mummy was always somewhere in the background and always around at bedtime.

In the summer and during the Christmas holidays, we visited the O'Keefes, my mother's family, in Wexford, an active port and market town on the southeast coast of Ireland. The O'Keefes were a prosperous merchant family, described in an early history of the town as Irish Papists. They were one of a few Catholic families who had managed to keep their land through the Cromwellian Settlement of 1649 and the later years of colonial rule.

My grandfather, William J. O'Keefe, was born in County Meath and had inherited the Wexford Maltings through his wife's family in the latter half of the 19th Century. He owned two steamships that exported grain to Dublin, Bristol, and other English ports. The O'Keefes lived in Faythe House, a large rambling place with stables and numerous outbuildings at the centre of the town. One of my strongest memories of the property is a fountain in the form of a swan that provided water to an ancient horse trough below. My grandfather died in 1924, before I was born.

Although I never met my grandfather, I remember Granny, a small grey-haired lady with a gentle voice and a nice smile. Her hankies smelt of lavender. Though overwhelmed by the endless chatter of her large family (everyone had a story to tell), she always listened attentively and never raised her voice.

After my grandfather's death, my grandmother Matilda and her three unmarried daughters, Molly, Eileen, and Maeve, continued to live in the family house.

We children loved these trips to Wexford – the expedition by car and the feeling of freedom without nurses and the restrictions of city life. Everything about the house was different, and we were curious children.

The large front hall was dark and sombre. Varieties of stuffed birds in glass cases and hunting prints lined the walls; the tall clock and the brass umbrella stand filled with a clutter of walking sticks reflected the image of a prosperous country gentleman. This was my grandfather's room. It was the only room that evinced his image and remained untouched until the house was sold.

I remember the walled garden where my grandmother grew roses, and Jim Nolan, a family retainer, who tended the vegetables and maintained the tennis court. We could view the harbour and smell sea breezes from an ivy-covered Norman keep; we explored the outbuildings and visited the horses. My aunts and uncles were horse people and rode to the hunt. My father had no love for blood sports and was known to make disparaging comments about *horse farmers* to the Wexford relatives. Our first riding lessons were on a tame donkey kept for our visits. I never enjoyed riding, but my sister Ann loved the sport, which she continued to pursue.

We loved these visits, exploring the maltings with its smell of fermented barley, and walking though the winding streets past slate-covered narrow houses and along the quays where my grandfather kept his ships.

Grandmother Matilda died in 1936. Some years later, Faythe House was sold, and the Aunts moved to the family cottage in Rosslare Strand.

THE WEXFORD AUNTS

olly, Eileen and Maeve, my mother's unmarried sisters, were known as the Wexford Aunts. They weren't to be confused with my other aunts – Daisy, an artist and businesswoman who was part of our Dublin family, and Katy, who married English army officer Jim McCaffrey and lived in Aldershot, close to London.

Rosslare Strand, where the Wexford Aunts lived after leaving Faythe House, was a small watering place where Wexford residents went for sea-bathing and golf. It boasted a magnificent stretch of white sand extending south to Rosslare Harbour where the ferry left for Fishguard in Wales. My grandfather had built a summer cottage there around 1920. Constructed of wood, which was not often used in that area, it was something of a curiosity and known quite simply as 'The Bungalow'.

We never stayed at The Bungalow. My mother preferred to rent one of the many cottages that lined the road behind the beach. I have fond memories of one with a leaky roof; the kitchen there smelt of damp clothes and smoke from the turf fire. Decorative shells adorned the gable door, and the cockles along the small path that led down to the road crackled under our feet. We appropriately named it Shell Cottage.

Another year, we stayed at the Cedars, a converted Victorian villa. The locals claimed it was haunted, but we never saw the ghost. My father, who drove us from Dublin, never stayed for more than a few days, leaving us at the mercy of the uncertain weather and the Wexford Aunts.

In those days, Rosslare was a quiet village with a small general store, a post office, a petrol station at one end, and a church and golf club at the other. Except for Kelly's Hotel, a pseudo-Edwardian brick building near the entrance to the village, and the rambling Gothic-style golf club, there were no buildings of consequence. A few residential villas had been converted to boarding houses. Apart from the cypress trees clustered around the golf club, the terrain looked windswept and bare.

❧❦

The Wexford Aunts were an incongruous trio.

Molly was the eldest Aunt, angular and imperious. She had sandy hair and smaller features than the rest of the family. She talked too much, smoked, strode rather than walked, and wore twinsets and tweeds even when she wasn't on the golf course. She had worked as a nurse in a London Hospital during World War I.

Next came Eileen, or Eily as she was called, a small timid person who kept in the background and did most of the cooking. A cleft lip gave her face a peculiar twist that puzzled us, though we never commented on it. She was quietly religious and attended morning Mass, but she never talked about God.

Maeve, the youngest Aunt, was lovely, with black shiny hair and a creamy complexion. Tall and elegant, she wore trousers and shorts long before they were popular among women. She must have been in her late twenties when we started visiting Rosslare. Her bedroom smelt of roses and fresh linen. She loved to paint and draw, maintaining order in the house with an artistic flair. I still wonder why she never left and made a career for herself in Dublin. Most of the men my aunts could have married were, like their brother Willy, killed in the Great War, or of the other persuasion (Protestants), which at the time would have been unacceptable.

Their social life centred around the golf club. Both Aunty Molly and Aunty Maeve were keen golfers, and Aunty Maeve often went to dances at the club. She kept her distance from us children but impressed us with her style and elegance.

❖

I'm sure my mother, who didn't swim or play golf, must have disliked these visits, although she never complained. Though she often went to the beach, she allowed us more freedom than we had in the city.

We made friends with local children, learnt to swim in the cold sea, and collected shells on the windswept beach. On chilly days, we explored the country lanes where fuchsias hung like lanterns and honeysuckle mixed with the scent of wild roses.

It was a treat to visit The Bungalow, but we had to be invited. The Aunts were uncomfortable with children, and we never knew what to expect. We usually went for high tea, which was served to the grownups in china cups, generally with biscuits or a little cake.

One particular visit sticks in my memory. It was a warm day with an overcast sky, one of those days when rain threatens but never comes. We had returned from the beach and were sitting down to lunch. My mother was in a talkative mood. Aunt Molly had invited us for tea.

"Remember to remove your sandals," she reminded us. "They fuss about sand in the house. I am meeting an old friend from Wexford for dinner at the hotel and will pick you up afterwards."

With brushed hair and clean hands, we arrived at The Bungalow. Aunt Molly appeared more agitated than usual.

"You'll have to wait for tea, my dog Laddy has just escaped up the Grange Road chasing the neighbour's mastiff," she blustered. "Be good and amuse yourselves on the swing."

The rain clouds had disappeared, and bright sunlight danced across the rose bushes along the garden fence. Delighted to be left alone for a while, we pushed each other back and forth on the old-fashioned swing that hung from a large oak tree in front of The Bungalow. My sister Ann was easily scared and screamed when I pushed her too high. I was a big tease, and this time I went too far. She decided to jump and landed on her face. Fortunately, the soft grass broke the fall, and she was able to stand.

"I need Aunty Eily," she cried, tears streaming down her face.

Eily, who must have heard her screams, dashed out and led her to the house.

"Let's see what's happening in the kitchen," she said. She turned to me and my youngest sister, Mary Rose.

"You and Mary Rose stay outside, you've caused enough trouble, I don't want to see you until teatime," she said in a more forceful manner than usual.

Thoroughly crushed and ashamed of our behaviour, Mary Rose and I decided to forgo the swing and sit tight until the crisis passed. It wasn't long before Aunt Molly arrived with a chastened Laddy, none the worse from his experience with the mastiff.

When I told her about the accident with Ann, she patted me on the shoulder and said kindly, "I know exactly how you feel. When Maeve was a little girl she fell from the same tree. I was the one who caused the accident."

✦·✦

That afternoon, the Aunts offered tea in the summer house, a gazebo-type building behind The Bungalow. Ann, none the worse for her bloody nose, had regained her composure and appeared ready to eat.

Eily excelled herself, providing delicious Welsh rarebit and homemade brown bread with gooseberry jam followed by her famous chocolate cake, all washed down with mugs of hot tea. Considering she grew up with household help, I wondered where she had learnt to cook.

Molly, who loved an audience, chattered away, entertaining us with stories of life in London during the

Great War. The one I remember most was about her time in a posh London clinic when the matron asked her to take breakfast to an important patient without giving his name.

"Perhaps it was just as well, since the man turned out to be Edward, Duke of Windsor," she said with a grin. "I might have dropped the tray."

Knowing her fascination with titles and tendency to name drop, I wasn't in the least surprised.

❧·❧

During World War II, we saw less of the Wexford Aunts. Petrol rationing and the sense of emergency at the time kept us closer to home. Molly and Maeve would occasionally visit us at Fitzwilliam Place, but it was never the same. For me, they remained part of childhood and the long days of endless summer.

At that time, I was totally involved in school and college, leaving Ireland to work in London in 1954. The Wexford Aunts were survivors from another time and place. I often wondered about the complexity of their lives, their dependency on one another, and how they worked to make things bearable within the confines of their narrow world.

FITZWILLIAM PLACE (1938-47)

939: Hitler invades Poland on 24 September. Britain and France officially declare war against Germany. The Irish Government maintains a neutral status, despite opposition in parts of the State. I was 11 years old and living with my family at 5 Fitzwilliam Place, Dublin.

We moved to Fitzwilliam Place in the spring of 1938. The street was a continuation of the south side of Fitzwilliam Square. Though only a short walk from our first house, it seemed miles away.

I was excited, not just about going to a new house but about the prospect of having more freedom, a park to play in, and somewhere to ride my bicycle. I remember running up and down the stairs with my sisters and looking at the trees in the Square from the fourth-floor window — the forsythia was already out. From the back on a clear day, you could see the barges on the Grand Canal and the distant Wicklow Mountains. Mummy was happy to be away from the commercial bustle on Baggot Street, not to mention the noise of the clacking trams. Aunty

Daisy must have been pleased, though I don't recall any of her comments at the time.

My father's practice had grown. There was a certain 'snob value' about moving to streets around the Square, which I didn't understand until later. This was the place where the Dublin doctors lived.

❧⋆❧

At first glance, our new house looked like all the other houses on the street, but on closer inspection, the subtle differences became apparent. It didn't have an elaborate fanlight, but the limestone Ionic pilasters that framed the entrance had elegant proportions. My parents argued often about the colour of the door, and my mother usually won. I remember it only as green, though often in different shades.

The hall was long and narrow but didn't seem so because of the large gilt mirror that hung above a black lacquered Chinese travelling trunk on one side. We called it The Duke's Chest, though I never heard the story behind the name. The hall smelt of beeswax and whatever flowers my mother decided to put in the pottery vase on top of the chest. These varied with the seasons, but it was never empty.

A large dining room opened off the hall at the back of the house and another smaller room facing the street was used as a waiting room for my father's patients. A two-storey wing at the back of the hall housed a small pantry, a bathroom, and an office for my father's secretary. An exterior door led to a walled garden and mews, where my father kept his car. During his office hours, my father urged us to enter the house through the mews.

Willie Marlow and his wife Maggie lived above on the second floor. We inherited them with the house. Willie was a portly red-faced man with a ready smile. His wife Maggie was as skinny as he was fat. Like the Duffs on Baggot Street, they never paid rent and my mother brought them food and leftovers.

My sisters and I slept on the fourth floor with our nurse Sarah, a freckle-faced girl who told good stories and made a fuss about my youngest sister, Mary Rose, at the time but didn't bother much with Ann and me. The main stairs continued up to the half landing and my father's office, which was out of bounds until we were much older.

I always considered the fourth floor where we lived with Sarah to be the best place in the house and, being the eldest, I had a room to myself. The wallpaper was spattered with pink roses. I had a view of the Grand Canal and the Dublin Mountains. My younger sisters slept in a large front room with Sarah.

I remember dressing on that fourth floor for formal dances and shivering in front of the small gas fire. On these occasions, Mummy was very nervous.

"Always remember what happened to your Aunt Maeve," she would say. "She was getting ready for a Hunt Ball, came too close to the fire, and ended up in the hospital with severe burns."

We often slid down the banisters and sometimes collided with my father and his patients as they came out of his office on the first landing above the hall.

I remember the elegance of the second-floor drawing rooms with their decorative friezes and chandeliers. The back room was my parents' favourite. It faced south and had a large window that was quite out of character with the house but made the room bright and cheerful.

❖

Aunty Daisy was still very much part of our world. She would help us with our homework in the first-floor waiting room after dinner. Years later, when I was cramming for the university entrance exam and needed help with the Irish language, she was unusually curt.

"How can I help you with a language that I neither know nor want to know?" she spat. "My best advice to you is to get a good grind, and I'll be happy to pay the bill."

She felt strongly, as I did, that learning the Irish language was a waste of time. I had to remember that her generation grew up before the Free State was established when the Irish language was not a requirement.

❖

I still visit the house at Fitzwilliam Place from time to time.

The Square still has its lilacs and laburnums, and the grass tennis courts are well tended, but the neighbourhood is different. The car repair business on the corner of Lad Lane is gone. A trendy restaurant has replaced the sweet shop around the corner. The doctors have moved to modern offices near the hospitals; their families live in the suburbs. Offices occupy the first floors of all the buildings, with the higher stories being converted to exclusive flats. The mews, in stark contrast to what they once were, are now attractive places to live. The booming economy of the Celtic Tiger has made preservation of these buildings possible.

❧•❧

Why do I keep going back? Is it just to see that it's still there?

I've never bothered to check in on the other houses we lived in. The house on Baggot Street was demolished in the eighties, and the house on Saint James' Terrace, where we lived during my college years, was more my parents' house than mine.

I suppose I visit Fitzwilliam Place because it brings back the magic of childhood, the security of family, and the excitement of growing up. I go there because so many other parts of the city have changed, but our old house and the nearby Square are almost the same.

It's been almost seventy years since we moved, and the house is still there, in better condition than I remember on my last visit two years ago. The brickwork has mellowed with time, but the trim and cast-iron railings are crisply painted. The door is yellow now.

"The only individuality you can give to Georgian row houses is to change their door colour and have beautiful window boxes," my mother always said.

AUNTY DAISY

Daisy, my mother's eldest sister, had been a part of our family for as long as I can remember. We never discovered why she came to live with us. She was just always there.

We had a *ménage à trois*, not in the risqué sense, but rather in the sense of having three parental figures instead of two; we had an additional parent giving us the best of her family support. Families were larger then and sometimes included a grandparent, a spinster aunt, or a bachelor uncle. My father adored Mummy, and Daisy was not a lonely spinster. My father and Daisy went to work while Mummy ran the household and took care of us children.

Margaret O'Keefe was an artist, businesswoman, feminist, and mentor. She was known to us as Aunty Daisy and to her students as Miss O'Keefe.

Daisy was the eldest of my mother's four sisters and also her father's favourite. Daisy and my grandfather discussed business deals together, and he often took her along when he bargained with farmers over grain.

She was the only one of my mother's sisters to ever talk about my grandfather, known to the rest of the family as distant and formal, although he had obviously been close to her.

The love of her life was said to have died in World War I, as did her younger brother Willy. She may have had other admirers, but we were unaware of them. Daisy was part of our household for as long as I can remember.

❧•❧

At twelve years of age, I began to be allowed to eat in the dining room. I loved the conversation, which ranged from local and foreign politics to art and literature. Aunty Daisy was on top of every subject and urged me to read the daily paper to broaden my outlook.

"You'll learn some history and understand what's happening in Ireland and other countries," she told me.

❧•❧

With no interest in sport, Aunty Daisy never commented on my success on the tennis court, though she insisted I take lessons in drawing and watercolour. She herself had studied at the Royal Hibernian Academy and had taken part in the Irish Arts and Craft Movement. Several local artists and poets lived in the neighbourhood, including the artist Jack Yeats.

When it came to homework, Daisy was there to help us with history, geography, French and English, but had no time for maths or the Gaelic language. She would sigh and say, "It's too bad to have such a requirement to enter the University."

She had a flat in Ely Place during the Easter Rising of 1916 and the War of Independence. We loved her stories of curfews and gunrunning, and her curiosity with the late-night visitors to Oliver St. John Gogarty's house across the street.

Mummy stayed at the flat when she first came to Dublin to have her voice trained and ended up meeting my father at a party given by mutual friends.

❖

Until the early 1940s, married women in Ireland were not encouraged to work outside the home, and single women were confined to positions such as companions or governesses.

An early feminist, Daisy had other ambitions. She gave art lessons at private schools and started a business with another artist friend, Gertrude Grew.

Gerty, as we called her, was born in Northern Ireland. A business-like person, she studied at the Belfast School of Art and received a scholarship to the Royal College of Art in South Kensington. With Aunty Daisy, she founded the Cluna Studio in 1923, and later they opened the Dublin Art Shop on Dawson Street.

Daisy felt strongly about making Dublin a more liveable city. She would often be found in the visitors' lounge of the Shelbourne Hotel writing letters to newspapers and various elected officials over cups of tea.

Opening Merrion Square for public use was her most important project. The Square is now an active public space for sports, concerts, art shows, or strolls along its tree-lined paths. She would have been pleased to see it.

Aunty Daisy's shop produced hand-painted greeting cards for Christmas and other holidays as well as

jewellery and enamelled broaches designed by local artists. My sisters and I worked there at Christmas and during school holidays.

A few years after Gerty died, Daisy became interested
in buying and selling antique furniture. She sold the
Dublin Art Shop and rented a small space on the south
side of St. Stephen's Green. Daddy joined her at auctions
in Dublin and at the country houses of the landed gen-
try within reach of Dublin. Though we had moved to
Clonskeagh, an inner suburb, a few years before Daddy
died, he continued to commute to his office in Fitzwilliam Place, which we still owned. Daisy herself stopped
driving into the city in her early 90s.

Aunty Daisy in Montclair, New Jersey, circa 1972.

When Daddy died prematurely at 53, Daisy was there for Mummy, looking after the financial affairs and restoring the family to a normal way of life.

After I finished at UCD Architectural School, she encouraged me to find a job in London while she kept the family together.

After I returned from my wanderings in Southern Rhodesia and South Africa, she and Mummy bought a small modern house on the coast near the village of Dalkey. She was always interested in my adventures – even my going to the United States earned her generous approval.

I married in 1966 and was living in Montclair, New Jersey. Two years later, when my daughter Margaret was born, Daisy came to visit. Despite difficulties with the flight, she arrived in good spirits. My husband Don organised trips to the auction houses in Manhattan, the Metropolitan Museum, Greenwich Village, and other places of interest. She adored my husband, who had a way with old people.

My siblings and I often wondered what it would have been like if Daisy hadn't lived with us. How would the family dynamics have changed? Would Mummy have been more forceful? Surely this is true: we would have been the losers.

EVA, MY MOTHER

I have a faded photograph of a beautiful child in a white dress holding her mother's hand. As the fifth child of a family of ten, my mother Eva spent more time with her siblings and family retainers than with her parents.

I always liked to imagine the encounter that led to that photograph ...

"I love my new dress," Eva says. "It has puffy sleeves and a long skirt, though our nurse Sarah insists I wear a pinafore."

"You can take it off for the photograph," says Sarah. "Now run off to the garden and remember to smile." Sarah is a country girl with red hair and freckles. She takes care of Eva, her three year old brother Ray, and Maeve, the new baby.

Eva scampers off, crossing the cobbled yard, past the stables and through the arched tunnel under the hayloft that leads to the garden. The familiar smells of horse dung and malt waft from the outbuildings. Malt is fermented barley, which her father buys from local farmers and sells to distillers.

"Never complain about the smell. Malt is the smell of money," Eva's mother had explained.

Eva is pleased that her older sisters, Molly and Katy, are away at boarding school. They like to ride horses and boss her around, but she misses Daisy, her eldest sister, who was back in Dublin as an art student.

Her brothers, Dick and Willy, are travelling with their father. Ray is still too small to play with. She sometimes feels left out, but today is different. Her mother has promised to take her photograph and let her help with the roses.

The garden smells of honeysuckle and spring. She sees the gardener, Jim Nolan, talking to her mother under the copper beech next to the tennis court. She hopes he will take her for a ride in his wheelbarrow. He looks towards her and beckons.

"Good morning, Miss Eva, aren't you the pretty one today? You won't be doing much work in that fancy outfit." he says.

Eva tells him she's having her picture taken.

Her mother suggests that Jim take their picture in front of the rose bushes. The rose garden faces south, towards the high, ivy-covered wall that surrounds the property, and is sheltered from the wind. Sun breaks through the clouds as they walk slowly to a stone bench beside the wall, which was part of the ramparts that surrounded Wexford town.

Jim focuses the camera and asks them to smile.

❧·❧

I knew her as Mummy, always there but never connecting, a haunting presence that floated through my childhood. A lovely woman who rarely raised her voice and had the ability to seem helpless and make others respond to her needs. Fortunately, people were there to do so, from my father and her sister Daisy to my sisters when she was older.

I was the one who passed her by, the one who never listened or asked the right questions. She was uncomfortable with small talk and any show of emotion. We talked in platitudes, about the weather and clothes, but rarely about people.

Was I more like her than I realised? Never bothering to intrude, to delve deeper and discover the person she really was?

More likely I was jealous of her composure, her beauty, and her relationship with my father. Weren't we both competing for his affection? Would things have been different without Daisy? I'm not sure. Would she have weathered the storm of early widowhood, coped with financial matters when my father died, had Daisy not been there?

My parents were openly affectionate but didn't always agree on how things should be done. When Daddy's fiery temper, mostly directed at things rather than people, would reduce my mother to silence, Daisy would often mediate, twiddle her long amber beads, make the appropriate remark, and order would be established. Without Daisy's presence, Mummy might have been stronger, but we, her children, would have missed out.

❧❦❧

Mummy sometimes spoke of her childhood, her elder sisters, her favourite brother Willy, who was killed in the Great War, and her mother, for whom she had a strong affection. She rarely mentioned her father.

"My older sisters went to boarding school in Belgium before the war," she used to say. "I had more time with my mother then and took singing lessons from Miss Devereux on Mary Street.

"We were a musical family. Molly played the cello and my brother Ray the violin. My family had parties during the war, when American soldiers were stationed in the town. It was very cheery. I remember singing a piece from *The Pirates of Penzance*. My sisters flirted with the young men, but I was the shy one and kept in the background."

Why she gave up singing after marriage, I will never know. She had a sweet voice and picked up popular music easily. She often took us to musical performances and later to the opera. I took music lessons, which turned out to be a lost cause. My sisters were even less enthusiastic. The fine German piano in Fitzwilliam Place was rarely used.

When Daddy died, my mother controlled her grief, which led to depression, of which I was unaware until years later. Ann and Mary Rose were at college and chasing boys, and my baby sister Esmay was still at school. I was off to London and a new life. Daisy kept the family going.

Mummy and I exchanged letters and cards, but our phone conversations were polite and stilted. I never told her anything about my life, and she told me less about hers.

However, our relationship started to change after I left for the United States in 1958 and returned some years later with my American husband.

She wasn't the least upset that we'd dispensed with the idea of a formal wedding in favour of travel. She adored my shy and formal husband.

Don Price was a lawyer and Midwestern transplant from Minnesota. He was wonderful with older people, and Mummy loved the attention. They went for short walks on the pier and around Dalkey Village. He brought her chocolates, and organised dinners at her favourite restaurant in the Dun Laoghaire train station.

***

Things were even better when I returned two years later with my son John. My mother loved babies, and John was an outgoing child who responded to her attention. On our first visit, we stayed in the small semi-detached house Mummy and Aunty Daisy shared in a new estate close to Dalkey Village. But after my daughter Margaret arrived, we found a bed and breakfast in the neighbourhood whenever we stayed.

After Daisy died, Mummy moved into Esmay and her husband Michael's new house, Corrigmore, in Elton Park. She had her own suite there and became part of the Rothschild family.

***

My mother, Eva, with her mother, Lilly, and grandmother.

Years later (Mummy lived to be ninety-two), when we were living in Montclair, New Jersey, I received an unexpected phone call from my sister Esmay in Dublin.

She was straight to the point. "If you want to see Mummy alive again, you'd better take the next plane to Ireland."

We spent our last night together in the elegant downstairs drawing room that had been converted to a bedroom. A relic of her former self, she was curled into a foetal position, but clearly recognised my voice and feigned a smile. I told her how much I loved her and offered food and water to no avail.

Her eyes closed in the early morning. She was finally at peace.

"Why didn't I listen? Why did I fail to question?" were my first thoughts as I let my tears flow.

THE BEGINNING OF MY EDUCATION

My first school was in a tall Victorian House on the corner of Waterloo Road and Baggot Street. It was a Montessori school, run by two maiden ladies, and known quite simply as Miss Meredith's. My memories of the school are hazy, except that we needed to be dropped off in the morning by my father or Aunt Daisy and picked up and walked back by the nurse or my mother in the afternoon. There was little serious learning and much of our time was given to play and interacting with the other children, some of whom turned up later at the convent on Leeson Street, which my sisters and I attended after the family moved to the house on Fitzwilliam Place.

We would walk there at different times every day, depending on the time our classes began. The streets around the Square were quiet, and the few cars always moved slowly. At the corner of St. Stephen's Green, a friendly policeman helped us cross the street. I loved those walks and often played hooky on the way home for a secret visit to the Smith's Lane sweet shop in a dark alley off Pembroke Street, which connected to the north side of the Square.

❧•❧

The school on Leeson Street was once a Georgian mansion built for a member of the Ascendancy during the colonial period. The building, with its wrought-iron balconies and splendid entrance, broke the continuity of the city block it sat on. We entered through the row houses on either side, which contained the classrooms. The nuns occupied the main building, which smelt of beeswax and incense. Large potted plants, possibly aspidistras with their shiny leaves, flanked the entrance. I imagined a hard-working lay sister dusting them once a week. Stained-glass windows framed the mansion's entrance. We gathered there for assembly once a week.

The Madams of the Sacred Heart was an ancient order founded in France by Saint Madeleine Sophie Barat after the Revolution for the purpose of educating the daughters of the Bourgeoisie. Their traditional black dresses had long voluminous skirts topped by short, cape-like over-blouses with tiny black buttons down the front. Their bonnets and veils were attached to pleated wimples that circled their faces. The wimples projected about two inches from their faces to keep their eyes averted from interested males on the Paris streets.

They had brought all of this with them when they came to Ireland.

In our teen years, we speculated wildly about life behind the green baize curtain that separated the school from where the nuns lived. Did the nuns wear bras? Or corsets in the case of the plumper members? And how about going to the bathroom with those voluminous skirts?

All things considered, they were an interesting group of women who stimulated our intellectual curiosity and commanded respect in more ways than we realised.

❖

I liked school but bridled at the discipline. The school uniform, a dreary navy-blue dress, was rough and scratchy, with pleats on one side and a red-braid trim that created a lopsided appearance. The white detachable collar was the one cheery note of this unfortunate garb. For sports, we had comfortable gym tunics very much like those worn by the girls in *The Belles of St. Trinian's* which we wore when we rode our bikes to hockey practice after school.

I made friends easily, asked too many questions, and frequently ended up outside the door, a typical punishment for misbehaviour.

The practice of rapping the knuckles had long since disappeared. Instead, we got extra homework and detention.

By my early teens, I had calmed down and become seriously competitive. Maths and science were neglected; I instead chose to put my efforts into the humanities. Besides French and Latin, we also had to study the Irish language, which we considered irrelevant. I'm not sure how we learnt anything – our teacher Miss O'Brion had a terrible time. We did everything we could to annoy her, from being late for class to looking out the window at the boys leaving their school across the street.

Looking back, we were fortunate to get a good education. In the early days of the Republic, the influence of the Catholic Church and the Government's preoccupation with reviving the Gaelic language greatly influenced culture and educational development. The Church, an international institution, allowed this small country to play a significant role on the world stage.

Terence Brown describes the situation aptly in *Ireland: A Social and Cultural History*. "If Britain had its material Empire, the Irish could assert their dignity in terms of a patriotism and spirituality that transcended the Island itself."

Sadly, this permeated every aspect of Irish life from censorship to anti-clericalism. Once the Free state was established in 1922, the Minister of Education set up a program mandating the Irish language compulsory in the National Schools and to enter the University. During my school years, I realise now if Irish had been optional, we might have respected it better and learnt how much it dictated the pattern of Irish speech and history. The Irish language is still compulsory to enter the University. When my grandparents on both sides of the family sent their daughters to be educated abroad this was not an issue, since Ireland was still a British colony.

DERRY, THE BROTHER I NEVER HAD

Aldershot, England 1935

The first thing I always remember about my cousin Derry is his beautiful long eyelashes. He was a blue-eyed little boy, who became my friend at an early age and later my confidant and admirer. He had all the advantages of a brother without the responsibilities of being one. We challenged each other from the beginning, shared ideas and people, and laughed and cried together.

⚜

I met him for the first time on a trip to England with my parents a few years before World War II. We were visiting Aunty Katy, her husband Jim, and their two boys, Derry and Roddy. Mummy often talked about her sister and showed us postcards of my cousins in front of the pyramids and in other exotic places.

Uncle Jim McCaffrey was a lieutenant colonel in the British army. They had just returned from a long tour of

39

duty in Egypt and were living in Aldershot, a town in Hampshire with a large military presence.

In the lead-up to the trip, I was so excited I could hardly sleep, but knowing my sisters were jealous, I tried to keep these thoughts to myself. Mummy bought me a brown tweed coat with a velvet collar for the trip. I felt so grown up.

Uncle Jim met us at Euston station. He was a burly, broad-shouldered man with thick horn-rimmed glasses. He said little but commanded attention. I got a peck on the cheek, but felt he was ill at ease with children. Years later, I learnt he had been involved in the shelling in World War I, which had left him slightly deaf.

Aunty Katy, a tall, elegant woman with light red hair and the strong features of her sister Daisy, gave us a friendly welcome. Her cheery manner made up for Uncle Jim's taciturn silences.

"Derry and Roddy are in the garden feeding their new rabbit," she said, taking my hand and leading me through the house into the garden. The boys seemed shy, though eager to show me their pet.

"His name is Abdul, after the rabbit we had in Cairo who escaped from his cage and just disappeared," Derry rattled off.

Roddy, a skinnier version of Derry, with a thatch of blond hair, looked sad and didn't say much. It took us a while to connect.

Derry, who did most of the talking, said he missed his friends in Egypt and didn't like the cool English weather. He seemed to know about things I'd never even heard of, such as what the Pharaohs put in their tombs and the number of slaves that it took to build the Sphinx. I thought he was a show-off, though was impressed by his knowledge and sophistication. I held my tongue.

The garden had a fishpond full of goldfish. It was late spring, and primroses grew under the pine trees. I remember liking the stucco, half-timbered Craftsman house and the curry lunch served with sliced bananas, raisins, and wafer-thin bread.

Uncle Jim took us to a military tattoo, which a member of the royal family attended. I think it was the Dowager Queen Mary. She wore a funny turban-like hat and lots of pearls. Despite pouring rain, the show continued.

⋖⋗

A few years later when World War II started, the McCaffrey boys came to Ireland. Derry, then nine, went to St. Gerard's, a lay boarding school for boys in Bray, while Roddy lived with us at Fitzwilliam Place and attended a day school nearby.

Roddy was quieter and more introspective than his brother, which made him a perfect match for my sister Mary Rose, who had much the same disposition.

I never knew who suggested their staying with us, whether it came from my mother or her sister Kathleen. Most likely it was my father's suggestion. With all the women about, he would have welcomed another male presence.

⋖⋗

Derry went to Ampleforth College, a boarding school in York, England, and later received a Degree in Engineering from Trinity College Dublin. When I was working in London after World War II, I remember he rowed for Trinity at Henley. After a brief stint working in the Fiji Islands, he returned to Ireland and married Cinnia Costello, who came from a large family in Dublin. They spent two years in Dubai and then moved back to Ireland. At the time, I was working in San Francisco.

Left to right: Derry, Mary Rose, Eleanor, and Roddy at Donegal.

When Mary King, my friend and roommate, and I were living on Taylor Street in San Francisco, I was surprised when Derry phoned to say he'd been offered a job in the Bay Area. I was excited and looked forward to getting to know Cinnia and their five year old daughter Ann Marie. They found an apartment on Telegraph Hill and quickly settled in. But Derry was restless, and, after about two years, the family returned to Ireland.

TENNIS WITH THE BOYS

One late afternoon at the end of May, when the lilacs were out in the Square, I put off studying for a test the next day and was instead playing tennis with my friend Miriam. We went to the Square every day after school, but rarely stayed late. On this particular day, my sisters had already gone home with the nurse.

I wasn't really focusing on the game. Two older boys were playing on the next court, and one of them had caught my eye.

After Miriam had to leave to go home, I delayed and fussed around with my tennis bag until the taller of the two boys walked over to me. He had large brown eyes, skinny legs, and a crooked smile. Nerves suddenly struck me.

"I'm Patrick and this is Sean. Maybe you and your friend would like to join us for doubles sometime? We come here most afternoons after school."

I could see he was as nervous as I was.

"I'll ask Miriam and tell you tomorrow," I mumbled, coming to the realisation I'd never played mixed doubles before and not even sure if Miriam would agree to play.

❧•❧

I was late for dinner that night but decided not to tell the rest of my family about my adventure in the Square.

By this time, I had started eating in the dining room. Things had changed, and my parents were more concerned with the evening news than eating dinner. Aunty Daisy hushed us so they could listen.

"Hitler has already taken over Czechoslovakia and now he's marching through Poland." The radio announcer's voice was loud in the silence.

Daddy seemed anxious to talk. "The question is, when will Britain come to its senses and declare war?"

For the past year, my father and Aunty Daisy had been consumed with the information coming through in the news. I had begun reading the daily paper and was aware of what they were talking about.

My father, who fought in World War I, had always been pro-British and never had good things to say about the Germans.

My classmates at that time were the children of the men and women who took part in the 1916 Easter Rising and the Irish Civil War. The events in Europe and other sensitive issues were never broached in history class.

My father gave me good advice on the subject: "If you want to survive in this country, never discuss politics, except with family and close friends, and even then you never know where they stand."

⋙•⋘

My life now revolved more and more around school and the Square. I still ate breakfast in the nursery with my younger sisters, though Sarah the nurse had long since left us to marry a policeman and live in Roscommon. She had been replaced by a Swiss-German au pair called Adele.

⋙•⋘

Friends seemed more important than family at this time of my life.

I could hardly wait to tell Miriam about talking to the boys and their invitation to play tennis together. She had three older brothers and told me they hit hard and liked to win. I liked to win too, not just at tennis but at school.

This drive to succeed always puzzled me, since no one pushed me at home. My parents rarely discussed homework and were not in the least interested in my success on the tennis court. Daisy was the only one who asked about my studies.

We all went to the Convent on Leeson Street now, leaving at different times. I walked by myself. Adele walked with my sisters, since their classes often started later.

⋙•⋘

The morning after my encounter with the boys, the hall was packed with noisy, giggling girls, eager to hang up their coats and jackets. It was stuffy inside, with light streaming in through the window over the entrance. The headmistress appeared, and the giggling came to a swift halt.

Mother Rita O'Donoghue was a large pasty-faced nun with steel spectacles and a bad complexion. Her sharp tongue and devious ways were feared by all. Not being one of her favourite pupils, I avoided her gaze and hurried up the stairs.

"Eleanor, you forgot to tie your shoelaces." A sharp voice sounded in my ear. "We don't tolerate sloppy dressing." Mother O'Donoghue always used the royal 'we'.

I mumbled a faint apology and scurried off to class.

❖

The test that I had neglected to prepare for the previous day was on the Irish language and was to be held that morning. Miss O'Brion was handing out papers, and I could feel worry creep over me.

Miss O'Brion was a tall creature with a large bosom that shook when she got excited and a slight twitch in her left eye. Normally we gave her a hard time, but this morning was different. The class was silent. This was a serious test, and we all needed to pass. The Irish language was compulsory for college entrance.

I looked around for Miriam, but there was no time to talk. I eventually passed the exam. In fact, I only just made it.

❖

Physical education was a half-hour break mid-morning when we exercised in the playground, rain or shine, under the guidance of Miss Nora Meldon, a muscular creature with a hearty laugh, who made us run and jump, usually to keep warm. Today, however, was different. A warm breeze whipped through the tall elms that encased the garden, and the smell of pansies drifted from the window boxes outside the chapel.

I looked around for Miriam to tell her about the proposed tennis game with Paddy and Sean.

"My brother Charlie knows them both," she replied. "Paddy is full of his own importance and a big tease. I'm not sure about Sean, but they are both good players."

I could see she was uncertain, although I pretended to ignore her and set a date for the game. We were reluctant to return to class after having been outside.

❖•❖

The next period was Latin with my favourite teacher, Mother Clare Hogan. She was short and chubby with a smiling face. It was clear she took great enjoyment from teaching.

"Will one of you girls please open the window. I know you'll hear the traffic, but I will just have to talk louder. Having the windows shut is too warm for this time of year."

I could tell she was perspiring heavily and wondered why the nuns didn't have summer uniforms.

She began class that morning with grammar and vocabulary and then we worked on translating a Latin text.

"This morning, we are focusing on the fifth chapter of Caesar's *Gallic War*. You have fifteen minutes to study the chapter, and then we will talk," Mother Hogan directed us.

I was distracted and didn't pay much attention to the lesson; the traffic outside, the bright sunshine, and Friday's tennis match seemed more important than a dead language. I struggled to make it through the class without blotting my copybooks.

~⋗•⋖~

Friday came around quickly. We had arranged to meet the boys after school. I was wearing my new white shorts and a yellow top. Mummy had a cold and stayed in bed. Adele was not well either.

When I knocked at the door, the room smelt of Vicks VapoRub and cough syrup. Mummy was propped up with cushions and sipping tea.

"Please bring me an aspirin," she said between coughs. "I have a splitting headache. You'll need to take your sisters to the Square. Adele is not well either and needs to rest."

My heart sank. How could I contact Paddy or Sean? I knew Paddy lived on the Square, but I was reluctant to call the house.

The sky was darkening as we reach the Square. Lightning streaked across the tennis pavilion. Claps of thunder followed, and the rain began to pour. There was no sign of Miriam or the boys. Mary Rose was terrified and wanted to go home. I grasped my sisters' hands and ran for shelter.

~⋗•⋖~

We saw Paddy and Sean on the tennis courts later in the week. They mumbled something about the storm, but never asked that we play again. Maybe it was just as well. I saw later in the sports section of the newspaper that they had won the All-Ireland Junior Tennis Championships.

Patrick went on to medical school and became a well-known orthopaedist. I'm not sure what happened to Sean.

CLOUGHEAST COTTAGE

It was already June and it hadn't rained for weeks. The tennis courts in Fitzwilliam Square were board-like and bare. The government had suggested water rationing. My parents and Aunty Daisy were absorbed in news from Europe and the possibility of war. I was more concerned about the results of the All-Ireland Junior Tennis Championships than world events.

We were in the nursery drinking Club Orange and munching on gold grain biscuits, our usual after-school snack. My sisters were listening to the record *Animal Crackers in My Soup* by Shirley Temple, and Adele had the day off to visit Switzerland for the summer holidays. She might not have been able to return if war had broken out. Mary Rose was preening in front of the mirror, imagining she looked like Shirley Temple. My middle sister Ann, whose hair was as straight as a board, was not impressed.

Mummy was about to speak, though my sisters weren't paying attention.

"We have new plans for the summer holidays," she said in a more animated voice than usual. "Instead of going to Rosslare, we've decided to rent a cottage on Carnsore Point. You may remember our picnics to the little harbour with the good bakery and the mushrooms we picked in the field beside the castle."

My sisters were excited and asked endless questions about swimming in the harbour, what clothes to bring and so on.

My emotions were mixed, knowing I would miss my friends in Rosslare and the tennis. But most of all, I was curious about why my parents had changed their plans. Rosslare was a fashionable watering place for Wexford, an important market town on the south-east coast of Ireland. My maternal grandfather built a family cottage there in the late 19th Century. We'd spent our holidays in Rosslare for as long as I could remember.

Maybe Daddy was the one who suggested the trip? It could have been that he wanted a break from my mother's family and friends in Rosslare, or maybe he just wanted peace and quiet from the gathering storm in Europe.

Carnsore Point was a remote and windswept spot, where sheep grazed close to the shore and the foghorns boomed on misty nights. I remember the jellyfish and seaweed on the harbour beach.

❧•❦

Two months after that discussion, we all squashed ourselves into the family car – my parents, Ann and Mary Rose, a picnic basket, and our dog Toto. Aunty Daisy would come later, bringing my English cousins Derry and Roddy McCaffrey, who were visiting Ireland for the summer.

Daddy was tense as we drove through a heavy downpour on the Bray Road. He was already complaining about the weather and the poor road conditions. When we reached the Glen of the Downs, the rain stopped, and a rainbow lit the sky. My sisters had drifted off to sleep.

We stopped briefly for a picnic lunch of sandwiches and thermos tea. The car smelled of stale cheese. It was a long tedious trip broken by numerous pee breaks in the woods or behind the tall hedges along the two-lane road.

We reached Carnsore Point in the late afternoon and stopped at the harbour before going to the cottage. The tide was low and gentle waves lapped against the pier. An ancient fishing boat encrusted with barnacles was stuck in the sand. On the other side of the cove, aggressive waves bashed against a breakwater stretching out to sea. Feathery clouds scudded across the sky, and wild fuchsias dotted the unruly hedgerows. We took off our shoes and raced to paddle in the lapping waves. The air smelled sharp and salty. Daddy waved to us from the top of the pier. It was clear to me that he was anxious to leave.

❧•❧

Positioned away from the harbour, a group of stubby gnarled oaks sat along the cliff, forming a barrier between the sea and the farmland that bordered the narrow road leading to the cottage. I could see it through the open window.

The building was whitewashed, with a thatched roof and red shuttered windows. A patchwork of fields extended behind it, which included the remains of a

Viking castle and the ruins of the Big House. A group of Jersey cows munched contently across the hedge that surrounded the property.

Mummy seemed anxious. "It's so much bigger than I thought it would be, I hope Mrs Walsh has opened the place up."

The cottage had recently been restored, largely by traditional standards. Mrs Walsh, a ruddy-faced woman with curly grey hair and a comfortable look opened the door. She offered us tea and showed Mummy around the house. We had already rushed upstairs to decide where we each wanted to sleep.

The downstairs area was a large, uncluttered space, with a kitchen wing at one end. Everything was painted white, like the outside. Homespun rugs covered the flagstone floor, and two beaten up, but comfortable, sofas framed the hearth, where a turf fire still burned despite the warm day.

"It keeps out the damp," said Mrs Walsh, who was eager to chat. "These old cottages can have a musty smell, even when they are restored, and the walls have been painted."

My mother nodded in agreement, sipping her tea, moving on to discuss what the only store in the village provided in the way of groceries.

❖•❖

We settled in quickly, swimming at the harbour beach and searching for crabs on the encrusted rocks that line the bay. I chased my sisters with the slithery seaweed and used a net to catch the tiny minnows that inhabited the pools at low tide. My parents sometimes took off to hike along the coast, leaving us in the charge of Mrs Walsh. When it was too cold to swim, we sat on the grassy verge making daisy chains and learning about the mermaids, who tantalise fishermen, and the bean sídhe, or banshee, who wails on stormy nights.

After a few days, Aunty Daisy arrived with Derry and Roddy. My older cousin Derry and I had always been friends. He was tall and good-looking with friendly blue eyes and the longest eyelashes. We joked about this, though I was secretly envious.

His younger brother Roddy was skinny and smaller with a thatch of blond hair. Derry and I tended to gang up against the younger children, taking off on our bicycles to pick blackberries and explore the countryside.

When the weather turned cold, we decided to construct a house in the field behind the cottage. Gorse bushes and driftwood provided the structural elements, and the holes were stuffed with old beach towels and whatever we could find in the attic.

We would sit there with our younger siblings drinking lemonade, telling stories, and wondering about the Viking castle and what happened to the family, who lived in the Big House before it was burnt by the Black and Tans.

⊰•⊱

The wind died down; the temperature rose. Mrs Walsh, who watched the weather like a hawk, announced at breakfast that we were in for a storm. No one paid her much attention. The grownups were relaxing in deck chairs, reading the paper. Ann, Mary Rose and Roddy were playing dominoes. Derry and I were reading in the grass some distance away. Then, I heard Aunty Daisy's voice, which seemed more strident than usual.

"It's almost 6pm. We must listen to the news."

Derry barely looked up from his book, a Victorian novel about the Great Fire of London. A few minutes later, Daddy went into the cottage and returned with our portable wireless set, a heavy battery-operated contraption. We sat quietly waiting for the familiar clipped voice of the BBC announcer.

"Here is the news. Two weeks have passed since Hitler invaded Poland. After a meeting in Downing Street this morning, September 3rd, 1939, Great Britain and France have declared war on Germany."

More followed on from that, but Aunty Daisy turned the radio off and disappeared silently into the cottage. Daddy was the first to speak.

"This will be a long one and different from the last," he said, looked wistfully into the distance. "Wish I was younger, but it's out of the question, and Ireland will be neutral this time."

I realised he was thinking of the Great War and his time in the trenches. Mummy, whose brother had been killed in the same war, remained silent and far away. I shivered, realising my childhood was ebbing away and feeling strangely sad. My thoughts swirled. *What will the future bring? A changing world lies ahead, and I will be part of it.*

Left to right: Ann, Mary Rose, Eleanor, Derry, and Roddy at Clougheast Cottage.

Clougheast Cottage.

THE MCAREVEYS OF COURTNEY HILL

I was having breakfast in the dining room with Daddy and Aunty Daisy one day while my sisters were upstairs with Mummy and the nurse.

My father hated chatter at breakfast, so he got straight to the point. "It's a blustery day with freezing rain. I'm already late for the hospital. Daisy will take you to school."

Once he left the room, I relaxed and looked at Aunty Daisy.

I had always wondered why we hardly ever spoke about Daddy's family. Maybe because they lived in Northern Ireland, which was a dangerous place. People didn't go there unless they had to.

I was a curious little girl, so I decided to ask Aunty Daisy about it after Daddy left.

"The history is complex, going back a few hundred years," she said. "Now don't bother me, you will learn all about it when you go to the elementary school at the convent."

Though shrouded in the mists of time, memories of Northern Ireland and my paternal grandparents are vague and distant. They came to Dublin once, when we lived on Lower Baggot Street. I was six and still going to Miss Meredith's Montessori School on Waterloo Road.

On the day of their visit, Spring had arrived – the lilac bush in our small back garden was in full bloom. I was bouncing tennis balls against the basement wall when Daddy called out from the back steps, "Come up quickly and meet your grandparents."

❧•❧

J.J. McArevey, my father's father, was born in 1855. He came from farming stock and was educated at St. Columbia's College in Newry. He started studying law, but on the death of his father took over the family business – making fine furniture, first in Banbridge and later in Newry.

He had one brother, James, who went to seek his fortune in Australia – without much success. His three sisters became Poor Clare nuns.

He married Theresa Downey, who came from a wealthy Kilkenny family, in 1880 and bought the late Georgian Courtney Hill House where he raised his seven children. Ambitious about their education, he sent the boys to Clongowes Wood College, a Jesuit Boarding School in County Kildare. Jack, the eldest, became a successful barrister in Dublin and died prematurely at 30. Harry, the middle child, took over the family business when his father died. The youngest, Bertrand (Bertie) – my father – became a doctor, specialising in ophthalmology.

J.J. was also ambitious about his daughters, sending his eldest daughter Clare to a convent school in Paris. She hated the school and became ill. The family only visited her once, and she subsequently died. Maud and Tessie went to Mount Anville, a convent boarding school outside Dublin. Maud became a nurse, married Leo McNally, had three children and died in childbirth. Tessie, the youngest, married Dick Flood, a Newry doctor.

Besides managing a flourishing furniture and retail business in Newry, J.J. was a member of the Newry Urban Council, chairman of the Newry Technical School, and chairman of the Brick and Stone Company. He was regarded as an important and trustworthy person in the town and was appointed a Justice of the Peace some years before he retired.

❧•❧

My grandfather was a shortish man with a wealth of beautiful white hair and piercing blue eyes. His wife, Theresa, though fat and plain, had a friendly face. They looked old and frail, but my grandfather gave me a strong handshake. My grandmother kissed my cheek and suggested we visit them at Courtney Hill sometime.

Mummy told me later that my grandmother had come from a wealthy family and had been legally required to hand over all her money to my grandfather when she married him.

❧•❧

The morning after their visit, Daddy, before he even read the paper, looked in my direction.

"I need to go to Northern Ireland very soon. How about coming along?" he said with a naughty grin.

❧•❧

A week later, we were off to Newry, the border town in County Down where my grandparents lived. I felt nervous and excited. Mummy had bought me a tweed coat with a velveteen collar, new patent leather shoes, and white socks.

Instead of taking the train, Daddy decided to drive.

Maybe he wanted to show off his new Vauxhall sedan or just be free from his busy practice.

After crawling for about two hours along the narrow one-lane roads, search lights flashed across the darkening sky. Daddy looked tense.

"We're coming close to the Border. Remember, no comments or chit-chat, just do what you're told, and keep quiet."

Soldiers with guns ordered us out of the car. They took Daddy inside a building close to the STOP sign near the Border and told me to sit on a bench outside. I remember feeling excited and a little scared.

Not long afterwards, we were climbing up the high steps to Courtney Hill House. Urns with huge aspidistra-like plants flanked the large, panelled entrance. Uncle Harry, Daddy's eldest brother, and his wife Marjorie greeted us at the door. They looked friendly and warm. Uncle Harry was an older version of my father, with the same blue eyes and sturdy build. Aunty Marjorie, a small pretty woman, greeted me with a big hug.

The living and dining rooms on the first floor of Courtney Hill House seemed huge and open. My grandparents were nowhere to be seen, but I felt their presence. Thick damask curtains shrouded the long windows, and a huge glass chandelier twinkled against the high ceiling.

I sat at the children's table for lunch with my three older cousins and their stern-faced French governess, Marianne. The rest of the family ate in another part of the room.

⤞•⤝

My three cousins, Naomi, Lorna and Margo, were typical teenagers, laughing and chatting together, trying to outwit the formidable governess. They mostly ignored me.

"Who is that old lady wrapped in a black shawl sitting by herself.?" I asked Lorna, looking across the room.

"Oh! That's Aunty Mary. She's a little crazy," she replied. "Last year, when Derick Flood, another cousin, was visiting, he pretended to be a priest and tried to hear her confession – she was completely taken in. How many sins could the poor old thing have dreamed up?" she continued with a giggle.

⤞•⤝

The next morning, Aunty Marjorie and Lorna showed me around the beautiful garden, which had a tennis court and large conservatory. It was terraced down to a meadow at the bottom of the hill.

Lorna was tall and slim with a mop of thick black hair and her mother's beautiful smile. She liked to chat.

"Next year, I'm going to boarding school in Dublin – just hope they have tennis courts," she said wistfully.

I told her I was starting tennis lessons and getting a racket for my birthday. Then we explored the back yard, with its beehives, hen house and garage. The next morning, we said goodbye and left for Dublin.

That was my first and only visit to Courtney Hill House.

—⊱•⊰—

Two years later, Naomi and Lorna came south and went to Mount Anville, a Sacred Heart convent boarding school outside the city. We had since moved to Fitzwilliam Place. They often stayed with us during school holidays. Mummy loved these visits. They likely provided a respite from the endless Shirley Temple pictures and songs.

I remember her saying, "Now I can take your cousins to more grown-up movies."

On this particular occasion it was *Gone with the Wind*, which I really wanted to see. Mummy considered me too young, which caused lots of family argument.

I went to see the movie some years later and still felt mad with Mummy.

—⊱•⊰—

The McArevey cousins moved in and out of our lives. Aunty Marjorie and Uncle Harry had another daughter, Valerie, in 1933.

After J.J. died, Uncle Harry continued to run the business. When he retired in 1946, Courtney Hill House was sold to the nuns, and the family moved to Dublin. The house was eventually replaced by a cancer research centre.

—⊱•⊰—

Some years later, my eldest cousin Naomi married her long-time boyfriend Jerry O'Conor, a friendly, gregarious barrister. We held the reception at Fitzwilliam Place. My youngest sister Mary Rose and my cousin Valerie were the bridesmaids.

A typical teenager, I was more excited about dancing in the front drawing room, having fun, and making new boyfriends.

❈

During my six years at Architectural School UCD (University College Dublin), I lost touch with the McArevey cousins but heard from Mummy that Lorna and Margo had married English officers stationed in Newry after World War II.

Left to right: Jack, Bertie, J.J., Claire, Theresa, Harry, and Maude at Courtney McArevey Hill House.

MY FIRST DAY AT BOARDING SCHOOL

efore Ireland declared its independence from the United Kingdom in 1919, the standard of public education was poor. Parents who could afford it either sent their children to private schools run by the church or abroad to France and Belgium. Two of my father's sisters went to a convent in Paris.

Daddy hated boarding school. As the youngest of his family, he was sent at the age of six to a Jesuit institution known for its learning and strict discipline. When we were small, I remember him saying, "That's something you girls won't have to worry about."

Years later, when I was almost fourteen, I astonished my parents, asking them if I could transfer from my day school to boarding. True, I was at a different age from my father when he had attended, and the convent school I attended, though private, was considered excellent. When Daddy asked me why, I came up with a weak excuse about run-ins with the headmistress and being bored in class.

"Maybe you've come up with a good idea. It will be a challenge, and I don't care for Mother O'Donohue, either," he replied, referring to the old Reverend Mother.

But there were other reasons. When my third sister Esmay had been born the previous year, the family dynamics changed. The house seemed too small. My baby sister was a lovely child and never bothered me, but I was a teenager and more interested in my own world than small children.

After her birth, Mummy and Daddy had hired Adele to help out with the baby. She came from the German part of Switzerland and gave us French lessons with a German accent. She always seemed more anxious to learn English than to impart her knowledge of French. She was tall and gangly with a pallid complexion but could make great scrambled eggs and scones. I hated her, and she disliked me.

My decision to change schools didn't worry other family members. Aunty Daisy, always my mentor, recalled happy memories of her boarding school days in Brussels and gave me her blessing. Mummy was totally wrapped up in the new baby and seemed to approve. Ann and Mary Rose, who were closer to my own age, said they would miss me, but they were probably delighted to have their elder sibling out of the way.

❖

The school year began in September. It was early autumn; the trees of the Square were starting to change and in two months they would be gone. My father loaded my luggage and other sporting gear into the family car, and we headed out of the city towards Dundrum, where the school was located.

I had a sinking feeling in the pit of my stomach. What had I got myself into? Had my independent streak gone too far? Daddy seemed relaxed and eager to talk.

"Don't let the nuns push you around. Remember, we will come to visit in a month's time," he told me.

Did he sense my anxiety? I wasn't sure, but I had no urge to talk.

In a short time, the high walls of the convent loomed ahead. Mount Anvil, a dignified Georgian mansion, was formerly the estate of an Ascendancy landlord. Several additional buildings had since been added to accommodate the school.

A porter directed us to the entrance for new arrivals. Daddy took my luggage out of the car and gave me a big hug. I could smell his tweed coat and special aftershave.

My eyes welled up. I couldn't think of anything to say, but he said it for me.

"No sad good-byes. Remember, this is a new beginning."

As he drove away, a small impatient-looking nun approached me from the building's entrance. My parents had sent my credentials ahead of my arrival, and the nuns knew to expect me that morning.

"The porter will take your case," she said in place of a greeting. "You'll be in St. Patrick's dormitory. Just follow me inside."

We entered a vast hall with corridors opening off on either side. It was strangely empty and smelt of beeswax and decayed flowers, though I couldn't see any.

"The girls are already in class. Our regular students always arrive a few days before the new arrivals," remarked the nun.

St. Patrick's dormitory was a huge high-ceilinged room on the top floor of the building with white-curtained cubicles opening off a central aisle. The floors creaked and a stiff breeze blew through the open windows. I shivered and hoped they would be closed at night.

A sharp cough broke the silence.

"One of our students, Kate Mulcachy, returned with a bad cold. Parents are very careless these days. The last thing we need is to infect the entire school," the nun said in a critical tone. She directed me to one of the cubicles. "I'll leave you to put away your things."

Except for the occasional cough from the ailing Kate, the dormitory was silent. I proceeded to unpack, wondering how I could fit everything into the one compact dresser I'd been assigned. Under the bed seemed like a good idea, and without further thought, I began to stuff everything, from posters, books, to small boxes of personal treasures into a corner under my bed. I was starting to feel quite pleased with myself when a piercing bell broke the silence.

"What's that all about?" I asked Kate, roughly pulling the curtains apart.

"Don't worry," she answered. "That's the bell for Assembly, or 'Notes' as we call it here. You better be in time. Just go downstairs, and you'll see a queue for the auditorium."

I was familiar with Notes, which we'd had at my Dublin school. I rushed out the door so as not to be late.

❧·❧

It was warm for September and the auditorium was stuffy. Light from the overhead windows flooded the hall. Prefects with blue sashes assigned our seats according to seniority. My neighbour, a tall girl with untidy red hair, was vigorously biting her nails. I looked her way and smiled but received no response.

The nuns filed onto the stage, their long skirts swishing behind them, their faces invisible behind their starched wimples. A small nun, obviously the Reverend Mother, opened with a prayer; her strong steely voice echoed through the auditorium. I concluded that she was the infamous Mother Bodkin my cousin Lorna had complained about.

"Keep in her good books and don't be fooled by her frail appearance," Lorna had said. I remembered that Lorna was always in trouble and had almost been expelled some years ago.

Since the school had just returned from the holidays, Mother Bodkin announced that Notes would not be given, but we must all proceed to the stage and be individually welcomed.

Normally, printed notes were given to students based on their performance during the previous week. The comments ranged from 'Very good' to 'Indifferent'. Rumour had it that too many 'Indifferent' comments could lead to expulsion. Besides the notes, students who excelled in certain subjects the previous week were given badges to wear on their uniforms.

Saint Madeleine Sophie Barat, the founder of the order of nuns who ran the school, had dreamed up this crazy system. Like it or not, it promoted hard work, competition, and above all, maintained discipline. There must have been other reasons why she achieved sainthood.

❖•❖

"I'm looking forward to lunch," said the red-headed nail biter, who had finally decided to smile at me after Notes was over. "My name is Siobhan, and you must be Eleanor, the new girl in our class. Sorry for being so horrible this morning. Let's go to the refectory. The food might be better than normal, since it's opening day."

The refectory, a large high-ceilinged room overlooking an open expanse of lawn and cedar trees, was a cheerful place. Sunlight streamed through the long windows and lay-sisters with starched white aprons bustled back and forth from the kitchen. I was ready to eat.

A chubby nun, the first I'd seen smile so far, intoned the grace and seemed to be in charge.

"She's really nice," said Siobhan, introducing me to the rest of the table, "and doesn't mind if you leave food on your plate or send you to the pantry."

This, I'd heard, was a punishment for those who didn't finish their meals.

The presiding prefect doled out the main dish, which appeared to be a watery beef stew with some overcooked vegetables. I felt queasy and understood then why students were sent to the pantry, but I decided not to complain. The meal ended with a wonderful deep-dish apple pie, which restored my confidence in convent cooking. I learned later it was only served on special occasions.

Despite the dreary food and threats of the pantry, school meals broke the tedium of a strict schedule, allowing us to talk freely, giggle about the nuns, and develop friendships. Siobhan, who seemed willing to show me the ropes, suggested we walk in the cedar grounds after lunch.

❧❦

"This is our free time," Siobhan explained as we walked around the grounds. "We are expected to be outside playing games or taking some form of exercise. I'm into field hockey, though it gets very muddy in the rainy season."

With memories of being bashed on the shins during various hockey games at my Dublin school, I was less than enthusiastic to hear this.

As we walked towards the playing fields, my body slowly relaxed. The air was clean and sharp, the Wicklow Mountains were etched silhouettes against the darkening sky. I was grateful to Siobhan for taking me under her wing but also content to be silent.

Returning to the school courtyard, I noticed a stone terrace punctuated with classical urns behind the main house; it led to a grove of elegant cedar trees. I questioned Siobhan about this.

"The area is off limits to students except in the early morning, when we are expected to run for thirty minutes before class. When the wind blows from the sea in winter, it can be pretty miserable."

Refreshed from the outdoors, we returned to the school building, washed our hands and went to the study hall. I was stopped by a tall nun with large prominent teeth, who was obviously in charge of allocating places to the newly arrived.

"Remember, no talking in the hall – not even a whisper," she said with a faint smile. "If you need to go to the bathroom, just raise your hand. I've left some books on your desk to read and study."

Despite what the nun had said, I could hear rustling paper and giggles coming from the back of the classroom. My neighbour, a small girl with green eyes and straight brown hair, kicked me and whispered.

"Don't worry about toothy old Sullivan, she gets involved in her own reading and often forgets what's going on." She introduced herself as Helen.

I kept falling asleep and hardly touched any of the books on my desk. It must have been the walk in the fresh air. A clanging bell announced the end of study.

"This is the last meal of the day and not too substantial," said Helen, as we made our way to the refectory.

Dusk had settled in, which gave the room a different ambience. We ate thickly cut sandwiches, washed down with mugs of milky tea and apples for dessert. At least the bread was homemade. I started to yawn.

"Wake up. I know it's been a long day, but there's still evening prayers and free time before bed. It's hard to doze in the chapel," said Kate, nudging me. She was thankfully well enough to join us for the evening meal.

❧·❧

The talk and giggling stopped as we filed into the chapel. Darkness had engulfed the building, and the nuns were already in their choir stalls. Once seated, we were led in a brief hymn by a tall, imperious-looking nun.

"That's Mother Campion – she's the music director and fancies herself as a conductor," whispered Kate. "She also gives piano lessons."

I was distracted by the beauty of the chapel and oblivious to the prayers that followed. The sombre Gothic space with its elegant and intricate stained-glass windows seemed more spiritual than the drone of surrounding voices. Despite the dim light, I could detect their brilliance and discovered later through Aunty Daisy that they were the work of Harry Clarke, a brilliant stained-glass artist.

❖

During our free time before bed, I grabbed a book from one of the study hall shelves and was about to sit down when two large energetic girls accosted me and proceeded to ask about my interest in music and other hobbies.

"Please, not now," I said, feeling totally exhausted and in no mood to cooperate. "Just don't put me in the choir. I have the voice of an underfed corncrake."

Without another word they went off muttering and shaking their heads. No doubt I had gone too far and felt there might be repercussions later. Mercifully the bell rang, and we made our way to the dormitory.

It was cold on the fourth floor; the windows rattled as I struggled to undress in the dim light.

"Fifteen minutes left," bellowed the dormitory nun, striding up and down the central aisle, switching lights off and on as she passed the entrance.

I made a pretence of washing my face, mildly cursing the icy water. The sheets were cold and the bed narrow, but it didn't seem to matter. With all the activity, there was no time for regret – that would come later. I had made it through the first day and that was enough.

Boarding school wasn't all roses. The discipline was tough. I suffered from chilblains from washing in cold water. But the teaching was good, and I made lifelong friends who followed me to university, and in some cases across the globe.

Kate went to Oxford and married a South African, and Siobhan became a successful doctor. I attended University College Dublin, studied architecture and went to work in London.

INCHANAPPA AND THE WAR YEARS

I had taken to reading the newspaper every day. It was 1940, and on May 15th, just a week prior, Holland had fallen to the Nazis. With U-boats sighted along the coast and the bombing of Belfast, the war seemed close. We sent care packages to relatives in London. My father, who thought Dublin might be the next target, decided to rent a house in Ashford, County Wicklow, a two-hour drive from the city.

"When the school term finishes, you can go there for the summer," he'd told us the previous day. "I'll join you at weekends and take my own holidays in August."

Despite the war, the prospect of spending the summer with the family in a remote Wicklow village was not exciting. I'd miss the All-Ireland Junior Tennis Championships and my friends in the Square. But things could be worse, my cousin Derry would be around for the holidays. We'd have our bicycles to explore the countryside and get away from the younger children.

❖

I had seen Derry quite recently. We attended Parents' Day at St. Gerard's, the boarding school in Bray where he would spend the later years of his schooling. His parents, unable to leave London, asked us to go in their place. The day was warm and smelled of lilac and freshly mown grass.

The boys looked gangly and awkward in their dressed-up clothes, but they shook hands and tried to make polite conversation. Derry, no longer the lonely little boy I remembered, seemed relaxed and confident. He introduced me to a friend of his, Brian, a tall skinny boy with thick black hair and a pointed face.

I wore a white linen dress and a Panama hat. We didn't say much, but the way he looked at me was exciting and different. Derry asked him to join us for lunch on the terrace. I remember the strawberries and cream and a shy young boy on his best behaviour.

⬥⋅⬥

"We should visit the house in Ashford next weekend," said Daddy, a few days after he had told us about his plans for the summer. "We can all squeeze into the car and pick Derry up in Bray on the way down."

With petrol rationing, cars were few and far between. The day was overcast and mild. Aunty Daisy decided to stay at home, since she had already seen the house. The thought of being squashed into the car with a bunch of rowdy children was not to her taste.

My father seemed happy and eager to tell us about Ashford. Mummy appeared happy and relaxed. As always, we had a picnic lunch of egg sandwiches, cold sausages, and a flask of tea.

"Ashford has no restaurants, except for the local pub and Hunter's, a historic inn, where you might get a meal," said my father, as we made our way through the Glen of the Downs.

The sun broke through the morning mist, and a herd of sheep straggled across the road. I tried to talk with Derry and ask about Brian, but my father monopolised the conversation. He wanted to tell us about the house in Ashford.

It was called Inchanappa and was built by an Anglo-Irish family called the Tottenhams in the middle of the previous century.

"Their descendants, Lucy and Clarinda, now elderly, supplement their income with rent from the house."

No one was paying any attention to his conversation. Derry, now much taller than he used to be, looked squashed and uncomfortable. I had cramps in my legs and the beginnings of a headache. My father, who must have sensed our discomfort, suggested that Derry and I make the next trip on our bicycles. With so few cars on the road, it seemed like a good idea.

As we approached Ashford village, the heavily wooded land rose steeply. My father told us to look for a Victorian gate lodge on the left-hand side of the road.

"The house is not visible from the road."

Curiosity and excitement replaced my negative thoughts. Derry and the younger children were silent. We made our way up the densely wooded avenue.

Smells of loam and decayed vegetation wafted through the car window.

The house was set on high ground with a sweeping view across the valley. It was built of limestone, in the manner of an Irish country house. The façade, with its projecting Ionic entablature, rose stark and grey against the horizon. A clock in the bell tower chimed on the hour.

The younger children, full of pent-up energy, fell out of the cramped car and chased each other across the lawn. Derry and I were anxious to see inside but comported ourselves a little more maturely.

He slipped me a note as we got out of the car.

"Brian asked me to give you this," he said with a naughty grin. "He thinks you're terrific."

My heart skipped a beat, and I was suddenly not sure what to say. We walked to the house in silence.

❖

Daddy turned the key. The place was empty and smelled of camphor and dust. Faded velvet curtains framed the long windows, and the chintz slipcovers looked tired and patched. However, the rooms had their own elegance.

Daddy opened the downstairs windows and commented on the lack of electricity. For some reason, Derry was excited by this and thought it would be fun to read in bed by candlelight. Daddy joked about using electric torches instead, but I could see he was distressed.

"Fire, my boy. It's so easy for a fire to happen in these old houses. If I catch any of you with a candle in the bedroom, there'll be trouble," he said, while looking straight at me.

Fortunately, the discussion was interrupted by the younger children rushing through the front door all red-cheeked and happy.

I must read Brian's note. Where can I find a quiet place? was the thought racing through my mind.

In desperation, I looked for the WC, a wood-panelled space with a tiny washbasin and a huge commode led up to by broad steps. I locked the door and took the note from my pocket. The message, written in bold handwriting on a page from a standard exercise book, was brief and formal.

I would like to know you better. Ask Derry to arrange a meeting.

Your admirer,
Brian

My thoughts were interrupted by a strident knock on the door. My youngest sister Mary Rose needed to pee. I slipped the note into my pocket and let her in. As we passed each other, she announced we were about to have a picnic lunch on the front lawn.

❦

I never answered the note but did eventually meet up with Brian at a party in Dublin. We tried to make conversation but found we had little to say. The magic had gone. I did, however, keep that note for a long time.

❦

We loved the old house in Ashford with its creaking floors, strange night noises and constant chiming of the belfry clock. Derry and I would sit up at night reading horror stories by Sheridan Le Fanu and Mary Shelly. We frightened the younger children with tales of a family ghost.

❧•❧

Roddy, the youngest of my English cousins, sometimes tells the story of how he was required to eat at Christmas dinner by himself on a small card table next to the larger family table because Aunty Daisy considered thirteen seated at the table to be unlucky.

"I was a shy little boy," he says with a chuckle, "not one to seek the limelight, and will never forget the mortifying experience."

This is something we still laugh about when we see each other now.

❧•❧

The McCaffrey boys lived with us during World War II and became part of our extended family. Derry returned to his boarding school in Bray and spent the holidays between Fitzwilliam Place and Inchanappa, while Roddy went to a day school in Dublin.

My mother, who didn't like the idea of us sleeping on the fourth floor of Fitzwilliam Place because of misplaced German attacks on the city, converted one of the elegant drawing rooms in Fitzwilliam Place into a dormitory. I remember a particular night, when Derry was home for the weekend and the younger children were asleep. The room seemed warm and stuffy, and neither of us could sleep. He wanted to talk about school.

"I really hate the miserable place, but coming here for weekends makes all the difference," he choked out.

His emotions were so close to the surface, I thought he would cry, but he never did. Boys were not supposed to cry in those days.

I pulled back the velvet curtain and opened the window. We sat in silence and looked across the quiet street, the Square's trees etched against the night sky and the streetlights casting shadows across the street.

Not far away, across the Irish Sea, towns were in darkness as people huddled in shelters waiting for bombs to fall. We were old enough to be aware of the danger.

Inchanappa House, Ashford, County Wicklow.

MY FATHER, J.B. MCAREVEY

We said goodbye in February. The day was cold and damp, the garden bare. Friends and relatives came to the house. The blinds were pulled and food prepared. Numb with grief, I felt nothing and held back my tears.

❧

He was too young to die, only fifty-three, at the height of his profession. His life had been a good one. He had enjoyed success in medicine, a happy marriage, and a wonderful family, and before that, the war in France and graduate work in Vienna.

He never talked about those years, and I never asked. *Why wasn't I more curious?* I was the oldest and perhaps the most like him. My sisters didn't ask either. Now, there's no one left to ask.

It's silly to cry after so many years, but I still do. I don't cry for Mummy and Aunty Daisy, who lived well into their nineties, but my father will always be young.

He would have liked sons, but he never said so. Fortunately, he enjoyed women's company and loved his four daughters. He was ahead of his time and from an early age encouraged us to make something of our lives – to be independent and have professional careers.

"You don't have to marry," he once told me. "You can be anything you want to be."

He often discussed the contributions of the female doctors he worked with and would have liked me to study medicine. When I told him years later that I wanted to be an architect, he shrugged his shoulders and said fine, but I knew he was disappointed. It must have irked him even more that I was the only one of his daughters at the time to take his advice and have a professional career.

❧•❧

As young children, we rarely saw him except at breakfast and sometimes in the evening, when he came to the nursery and tucked us into bed. He was always more relaxed at the end of the day, inquiring first about our school days and always finishing with made-up stories of goblins and fair maidens chased by witches in dark forests. They were more funny than scary and could have kept us awake at night, but I don't remember that they did.

❧•❧

Life wasn't all sweetness and light, though. My father had a dark side, and when his temper flared up, we learned to keep out of the way. His outlet was golf, which he played every Sunday morning after Mass.

He was of the old school and a stickler for manners. At breakfast, where Aunty Daisy often presided, since my mother rarely appeared before noon, he demanded peace and quiet. Even at weekends, we could never appear in robes and slippers, and heaven forbid if you were wearing curling pins or rollers. Maybe that was why Mummy decided to stay in bed.

At weekends, he loved to hike and often took us with him; Mummy and Aunty Daisy rarely came. On Sunday after lunch, we often explored the Wicklow Mountains from the vale of Glendalough to the bleak bog country along the Military Road. The going could be rough as we scrambled along mountain paths in pouring rain, but we got used to the elements, helped by stories of the Civil War and the Black and Tan raids before Ireland became a free state. When we tired of the mountains, we would drive to Dun Laoghaire and walk along the pier, where waves crashed against the granite walls and cormorants kept watch around the lighthouse.

❧•❧

I was in architectural school when he became ill. The family had moved from Fitzwilliam Place to Clonskeagh, an older suburb, during my first year of college. I still slept at home but spent long days and nights in the studio. On one of my rare weekends at home, I noticed my father's worried face and heard my mother and Daisy muttering about doctor's appointments.

Preoccupied with work, I didn't think further about it, until sometime later my mother told me that my father was having an operation the following week.

"What is it all about?" I asked her and was politely told I needn't worry.

My family disliked talking about unpleasant things, especially those concerning illness or death. Maybe they did this to protect us – a ridiculous notion considering I was twenty-two years old. We were taught to grieve in silence and keep a stiff upper lip.

❖

Eventually I discovered from Aunty Daisy that my father had colon cancer. In those days the 'Big C' was always mentioned in hushed tones. If a member of your family was struck down, you just told friends they were ill. My father quietly went on with his work, and we waited.

❖

He took a long time to die – almost two years – but lived every day to the fullest. A trip to London with my mother for a medical conference kept him going for a while. I remember the funny stories he told about the participants.

He continued Sunday walks on the pier with my mother and Aunty Daisy as long as he could. In his last year, he needed people around him more than ever, especially his colleagues from the hospital. He would take

Mummy out to dinner and order champagne and oysters, one of the few things he could eat.

❖

My work was a distraction. I avoided coming home, even for Sunday lunch. I went on a hiking trip in Wales with a group of students the September before he died and was plagued with guilt. I dreaded making phone calls home. Mummy seemed quite composed when I questioned her about my father's health.

"He is much the same," she would say, and then ask me when I was coming home. Maybe denial kept her going.

❖

One day, he phoned me and asked me to pick him up at the house. I remember it being a cold, damp evening; the trees lining the Square were dark and forbidding, their branches etched against the darkening sky.

The illness had taken its toll. He looked frail and vulnerable. I held back tears and helped him down the steps. This would be his last trip to his office.

❖

He died a month later. I kept my composure at the funeral, but when we returned from the cemetery and all the guests had gone, I closed my bedroom door and cried myself to sleep.

❖

Left to right: Daddy, Mummy, Esmay and Aunty Daisy, circa 1950.

But family obligations forced me to face reality. While Aunty Daisy took care of Mummy, and with Derry, who was my eldest male relative at that time, out of the country, Roddy and I had legal and business matters to sort out.

AFTER UNIVERSITY

After I finished Architectural School in 1951, I badly needed to get out of Dublin and ventured across the water. London was dreary, grey, and full of unfinished, war-damaged buildings, but I was excited and ready to take whatever came along. Jobs in architecture were hard to find, especially for women.

I ended up working as a draughtsman in a government office at Bush House on the Strand – not very inspiring, but the people were friendly. I could also explore London on the Underground or my bicycle.

❊•❊

Biking to work from Barnes Bridge, a suburb near Richmond where I boarded with my cousin Stelle and her husband Ronnie Harvey became a daily adventure.

In those days, the city was subject to a dense fog with an unhealthy air quality. Buses crawled through the crowded streets, sometimes so slowly that I could ride alongside them. I worked at Bush House for almost a year (1951–52).

❖

One cold wet day on my way to work, I caught sight of a colourful poster of a sunlit beach and palm trees which made me think twice.

What am I doing in this horrible climate? I thought to myself.

I'm not saying this was the prime motive for following my McArevey cousins to Africa the following year, but it might have helped me on my way.

IN THE LAND OF BANTU

*W*hen I graduated from architectural school in 1951, the economies of Britain and Ireland were severely depressed. Many young professionals were forced to emigrate. Since two of my older Irish cousins were already in Africa, I decided to follow in their footsteps.

I said goodbye to my Dublin family and boarded a Cunard liner at Southampton en route to the port of Beira in Mozambique. The train journey from Beira to Salisbury (now Harare), in the former British colony of Southern Rhodesia (now Zimbabwe), took eight hours.

This is where my story really begins.

◄◆►

The train to Salisbury arrived late. I looked through the grubby window at the noisy crowd, waving their hands and pushing their way towards the train. People from all walks of life – women in floral frocks, weather-beaten young men in khaki shorts, and tall men wearing turbans – mingled together.

Through the open window, the air reeked of sweat and dust. I felt nervous and confused.

My head ached.

Had my adventurous spirit finally gone too far? With some difficulty, I extricated my heavy suitcase from the overhead rack and descended cautiously onto the crowded platform.

After the humidity on the coast, the air seemed hot and dry. I couldn't believe that several weeks had passed since the boat had left Southampton. My travelling outfit, a very unsuitable tweed suit, began to itch. I should have worn a light dress. Fortunately, the crowds dispersed quickly. I decided to stay in one place and try not to look hot and nervous.

Aunty Katy and Uncle Jim's old army friends, Tony and Margaret (Mushi) Badman, had agreed to meet me getting off the train. I didn't know much about the Badmans, except that Tony was an army dentist and that he and his wife had retired to Southern Rhodesia after World War II. Aunty Katy, one of my mother's older sisters and a favourite of mine, liked them, and that was enough for me.

I could see a tall man of military bearing emerge from the entrance to the railway station. He appeared to be searching for someone, and eventually turned his gaze in my direction. I took a chance and waved. As he came towards me, I observed his straight-backed figure, ruddy face, and small moustache. He was dressed in well-pressed cotton trousers and an open-necked long-sleeved shirt.

"You must be Katy's niece, Eleanor. I'm Tony Badman." His crisp English accent was reassuring and kind.

"Is that all the luggage you have?" he continued, looking at my overstuffed suitcase. I told him my trunks had been shipped. "Let's get out of here, you look exhausted."

He smiled and took the heavy case. Outside the station, a chaotic mix of bicycles, handcarts, and pedestrians filled the square. Warm and pungent air, a mix of tobacco and flowers from the surrounding trees, floated above the jostling crowd. I could see an open-air market on one side of the parking lot and a huge barn-like structure on the other.

"Twice a year, farmers from all parts of the colony come here to market tobacco. Business is quiet now, but once the bidding starts, this place becomes a whirl of activity," Tony told me.

By this time, I had developed a pounding headache and barely heard what he was talking about.

❖•❖

As we left the crowded market and passed through a large industrial zone, the landscape changed. The narrow street became a tree-lined boulevard with elegant low-slung bungalows on both sides, their weathered roofs barely visible among the vines and foliage. The air became fresh and fragrant. My headache began to fade.

"We are now in the Avenues. I love this part of the city. It's considered Salisbury's oldest and most beautiful residential area," said Tony. He continued, pointing to the canopy of delicate purple foliage above the street, "The jacaranda trees give the neighbourhood a special character.

"It's a perfect tree for the hot veldt of East Africa. Cecil Rhodes and his friends did us a favour planting them around the city. We wanted to live here, but the houses are too large and expensive to maintain."

After a bit of driving, the boulevard became a dirt road. Tall eucalyptus trees now replaced the jacarandas.

"We call them blue gums here," said Tony.

Their distinctive scent was already floating through the open car window.

As he talked, I noticed groups of small, one-storey concrete-block houses scattered among the trees. Some were still unfinished; their white-washed walls, tile roofs, lack of traditional verandas and manicured gardens seemed more suitable for a London suburb than the untamed veldt of southern Africa.

"This is Marlborough and bears no resemblance to its namesake in England," said Tony with a grin. I was too polite to comment on the British obsession of using English place names in colonial outposts.

"You're late and should have phoned," said his wife, Mushi, by way of greeting. She was a small roly-poly woman dressed in a colourful silk muumuu and wearing silver slippers that matched the colour of her lacquered hair. She feigned a smile, though I could still see her irritation.

"How about some tea?" said Tony, "Eleanor is exhausted and ready for a nap, and I could do with a drink."

The large living-cum-dining room was comfortable in a formal way, with a light beige carpet, off-white walls, and a huge picture window facing the small, manicured garden.

My limbs ached. I needed a bathroom and somewhere to rest. Mushi, not upset when I begged off tea, led me to a small room at the back of the house. All I remember is closing the blinds, undressing, and collapsing on the hard narrow bed.

Eventually, someone knocked on the door. It was almost 6pm and already dark. I'd forgotten that there was no twilight near the equator. Tony had mentioned a 7:30pm dinner with their daughter and her husband.

I quickly washed my face and looked for a light dress. My clothes, not yet unpacked, were wrinkled, but it didn't bother me. I was rested and curious to meet the rest of the family.

When I entered the living room, the guests had already arrived. Stella, Tony and Mushi's daughter, and her husband Ralph Smith were young, newly married, and recent newcomers to the colony. Stella, a thinner, smiling image of her mother, was a nurse at the local hospital. Ralph, an engineer with the Rhodesian Railways, was a thin gangly man with friendly eyes. I told him I was an architect.

"How is building in the Colony?" I asked him.

"Construction is booming," he replied, "but being a woman could make things difficult. The early Colonists are old-fashioned, but the recent ones would be delighted to have someone like you."

Tony offered drinks. He and Mushi had sherry. I joined the younger people in a whiskey sour. A long blue silk curtain shut out the night, and the smell of curry wafted from the kitchen. It seemed a long time since my sandwiches on the train.

Dinner was served by a young African man named Zebadiah. Tony congratulated him on the quality of the meal. Everyone was hungry, and the conversation flowed.

Stella and Ralph were attentive and curious as to how I could find a job. I had relaxed enough to ask about prospects and where to start. They were enthusiastic and had contacts with some local architects.

Ralph asked about my work in London and said he might be able to arrange some interviews for me, but they would have to take place in Salisbury. Tony, who had a dental practice there, suggested I drive with him, which would give me time to look around and walk to his office.

"The business area in Salisbury is compact," said Tony. "You can always rest on one of the benches in Cecil Square or have coffee at Meikles."

I learned later that this was the most elegant hotel in Salisbury. It became a favourite meeting place when I needed a rest.

I was grateful for their suggestions and already thinking about what I should wear. Women in London had started to wear trousers to work, though I wasn't sure if that would be accepted here.

Maybe Stella can give me some advice? I thought to myself. But this was not the time to ask. I was getting sleepy. Tony yawned and looked at his watch.

Stella and Ralph said they would arrange to meet me for lunch the following week.

❧

The next morning, I woke to chattering birds and a soft breeze drifting in gently through the window. A tap on the door announced the arrival of tea. The small tray outside held a white china cup and two Marietta biscuits. I was reminded of Dublin and the many cups I took to my mother on cold winter mornings.

After a warm bath, I dressed quickly. Mushi was busy watering some indoor plants, and Tony was nowhere to be seen. I remembered he had a small dental practice in Salisbury and must have gone to work.

❧

At breakfast, Mushi lectured me on the problems of living at a high altitude. "You may get breathless even walking up the stairs. To stay healthy, you must go to sea level at least once a year."

I knew about altitude sickness but decided to say nothing, wondering how many of the country's native inhabitants ever made it to the coast.

The day passed quickly between unpacking clothes, writing notes to my family, and trying to avoid Mushi's endless chatter.

❧

The following morning, I was up early and ready to leave with Tony when he headed off to Salisbury. As we drove through the Avenues, he commented again on the low-slung bungalows with their porches and richly planted gardens.

"You should try to live in this neighbourhood if you can. Many of the larger homes have rooms for rent. It's so convenient. You can walk or take a bus to the centre of town."

I was excited and more determined than ever to get a job. Tony talked about local customs and places to visit when I explored the city. When I asked about communicating with the Africans, he assured me that most of them understood English, though it was often hard to understand them.

"The Bantu language is the one most commonly used in this part of Central Africa," he said. "Remember to stay around Cecil Square and don't venture south of Rhodes Avenue.

"The country may seem peaceful, but I've sensed restlessness among the Africans in recent months. We must realise that the colonial era is coming to an end."

He said this wistfully, and I felt his nostalgia but didn't want to engage in a political debate on the future of Britain's colonies. He must have sensed my thoughts and quickly changed the conversation to more practical topics.

"Meikles has public phones. You can always get tea or coffee at a modest price, so don't be put off by its pretentious interior," he said. "Come to my office whenever you like. You can rest there and wait until I'm finished with my patients."

❧•❧

Work began early in Salisbury. By 8am, the city was humming with activity. Bicycles, handcarts and small cars jostled along the broad tree-lined streets. The air was rich with unfamiliar smells, a combination of fragrance from the gardens in Cecil Square and exhaust from the cars and trucks. I quickly identified Meikles Hotel, a dignified colonial-style building with a red-tiled roof surrounded by palms and bougainvillea. Since it was too early to make telephone calls to the architects Ralph had recommended, I decided to take a walk and get a feel for the city.

As I left the Square with its wide streets, well-kept public buildings and manicured gardens, the ambience changed. Small stores selling everything from cooking pots to food and vegetables lined the narrow streets. Smells of curry and unknown spices drifted through the open doors.

The crowds increased, with more Black faces than White. It felt good to be anonymous again, much like London but more exciting and unpredictable. Nobody bothered me, but I remembered Tony's advice and kept a firm grip on my handbag. Here I was a minority, a White face in a Black country – a different world.

It took a while for me to get out of the market area and return to the Square. The temperature soared. I was totally exhausted and needed a bathroom. The only option was to head for Meikles.

❧•❧

I entered the lobby with some trepidation. The huge space was cool and refreshing. Fans whirred overhead.

101

A turbaned waiter in a long white tunic led me to one of the many small glass-topped tables grouped around an ornate ceramic fountain. I ordered tea and biscuits, and the waiter directed me to the bathrooms.

Though it was still mid-morning, the hotel hummed with activity. Men in light business suits mingled with farmers in shorts and bush jackets around a bar at the end of the hall. The leather furniture, highly polished floor scattered with Persian rugs, and stuffed animal heads echoed the colonial past. Above the hum of conversation, I could hear a tinkling piano. The air smelled of tobacco and beeswax.

A casually dressed young man, seated at a nearby table, was looking toward the entrance. As he scanned the room, we made eye contact. I felt young and vulnerable. Was he an agent from some tobacco company or a farmer here for business? Or was I looking for a new boyfriend?

Thoughts of Michael, a young architect I had loved and left in Dublin, came back to haunt me. But this was not the time for second thoughts. I was in Africa, a long way from home, and I needed a job.

First, I had to find a telephone. The hotel concierge was happy to point me in the direction of the hotel phone.

I rifled through my handbag for the list of architects given to me by Ralph Smith, and a card given to me by a salesman I had met on the boat who said that he had done business with Montgomery & Oldfield, an architectural firm that had recently won a competition. I decided to call them first.

Nick Montgomery, one of the partners, answered the phone. His voice was crisp and articulate, a London voice with regional overtones. I introduced myself and explained that I was in the city calling from Meikles and looking for a job.

"You're so close to our office, why not come here?" he replied. "We're on the second floor of the Goldsmith Building on Cecil Square, just around the corner."

I felt excited and nervous, but Nick sounded nice. The cotton dress I had bought in London was positively stylish compared to the old-fashioned frocks worn by the women at Meikles. I was prepared for an impromptu interview.

I had no trouble finding the office. The Goldsmith Building was one of the many concrete block structures with two-storey porches that surrounded part of Cecil Square. The first-floor porch formed a colonnade with access to small shops, with offices located off a covered porch on the second floor. A lanky African boy in a white shirt and ragged-looking shorts sat on a wooden crate outside the office. He was reading and hardly noted my presence. Jazz music wafted out of the window. I rang the bell. A tall bespectacled young man with spiky blond hair answered the door.

"My name is George Pink. You must be the Irish girl Nick just talked to. Why don't you wait here," he said, leading me to a small reception space with two Eames chairs and a glass coffee table piled high with periodicals.

An elderly lady with frizzy hair was busy typing and barely raised her head to acknowledge my presence. I sat down and waited.

Suddenly, a door banged open, and a slight, beetle-browed man with piercing brown eyes swept into the room. Nick Montgomery exuded energy. He talked fast, moved fast, and as I learnt later, never missed a trick.

"Let's go into the drafting room. It's easier to talk there," he said, looking at the typist. It seemed odd that he never introduced me. He scanned my résumé, glanced at the drawings in my portfolio, and nodded without much emotion before speaking.

"We've just won a competition for a school and badly need help with the residential stuff. Let me talk to Peter."

He ushered me into the drafting room and rushed away somewhere, presumably to fetch Peter.

❧•❧

I sat on the edge of a hard chair in the room and found it hard to relax. George Pink was sitting at a drafting table at other end of the room. The background music continued. It sounded like John Coltrane, but I wasn't sure.

After a few minutes, both men returned. Peter Oldfield was pale with a mop of black curls, blue eyes and a cherubic face; his body was soft, though by no means fat. He wore a yellow bow tie, faded beige cords, and Hush Puppies. Nick introduced us.

"How do you like our primitive surroundings – very different from London, eh?" Peter said, with an impish grin.

Before I had a chance to reply, he began talking about Montgomery & Oldfield's recent projects, which, except for the school, were mostly residential.

"I'm sure you've never seen a house built on top of an anthill," Peter rushed on. "The ants are dead, but they compact and make a good foundation."

Nick excused himself and left us alone. Peter continued to discuss the local architecture. I wondered whether he enjoyed talking about himself or was just putting in time before sending me on my way.

"People here are conservative and scared of modern design. It's understandable, since they just haven't seen much. We have to make them excited," he said, showing me a recent model of his work, a small house on stilts with lots of glass and an angled roof.

Looking at my drawings, he commented on my working at the London County Council.

"It's a good place to get experience, but you were wise to leave – nothing but government buildings. You'll get broader experience here, site work and that sort of thing. When would you like to start?"

"How about Monday," I replied, trying to sound calm and professional.

He offered me a monthly salary, which seemed fine. It occurred to me later that I should have explored the cost of living in the colony before accepting, but somehow it didn't seem to matter.

"You'll work with George. He's a cheerful chap, though his music may get on your nerves. Don't worry about Mrs Briggs, our part-time secretary. She's not as formidable as she looks. Jonah, the young African lad outside, runs errands, keeps the place clean, and makes excellent tea."

❧•❧

I worked with Montgomery & Oldfield for almost two years and found accommodation in the Avenues. I kept in touch with the Badman family and made friends with young people who had come, like I had, to find work and escape from the dismal conditions at home. But change was inevitable. We were living in a fool's paradise. The colonial system was breaking up. We realised that Africans would and should be in charge of their own destiny.

In 1965, the Conservative White Government made a Unilateral Declaration of Independence from Great Britain, and the colony became the unrecognised state of Rhodesia. The state endured fifteen years of bloodshed and carnage, which culminated in a peace that established universal enfranchisement. In 1980, Rhodesia was renamed Zimbabwe and joined the Commonwealth of Nations.

Eleanor in Lusaka, Northern Rhodesia, now Zambia.

Eleanor on safari in Southern Rhodesia, now Zimbabwe.

ROMANCE, ENDURING FRIENDSHIP, AND A WEDDING IN NYASALAND

I quickly settled into my new job. Montgomery & Old-field was a bustling place. The competition they'd just won was to design and build the multi-racial university in Salisbury; George Pink still played his cool jazz and Jonah still made us tea, but Nora Musto, a friendly young woman, eventually replaced the crabby Mrs Griggs at the front desk.

❧•❧

One day, Nick Montgomery, more relaxed than usual, breezed into the office, giving me a big grin.

"How about designing Henry Williams' house in Marandellas? Peter and I are up to our eyes with this competition. You've heard me talking about what Henry's looking for – a red-tiled Colonial, but with a modern touch ..."

I knew recapturing the colonial past was not Nick's cup of tea. Even knowing this commission was a cast-off, I was pleased to be given more responsibility. Besides, my personal life had changed recently. I'd fallen seriously in love – so magical and wild, I couldn't believe it had happened.

❧•❦

Almost three weeks before that conversation with Nick, Daphne Littledale, a friend from Dublin working in Salisbury, had invited me to a weekend party at Leopard Rock, a famous resort in the Umtali Mountains. She suggested I should bring formal clothes.

Part of the weekend was a rugby match between Southern Rhodesia and a newly formed South African team, the Springboks. Daphne was a big sports fan who knew one of the players and got us free tickets. I'd once followed rugby as a student in Dublin but was never a serious fan.

Tired from working non-stop since starting at Montgomery & Oldfield, and needing a break, I accepted the invitation for this adventure. Leopard Rock was incredibly beautiful, set in the lush foothills of the Umtali Mountains; what had once been a shooting lodge was now a luxury hotel. In the evening, we ate delicious food and danced with the young athletes.

I never knew what made Patrick pick me out of the crowd. Maybe it was my elegant turquoise dress. But the reason didn't matter. The attraction was mutual.

Patrick was tall, attractive and brown-eyed; he was older than his teammates. He used to play serious rugby but had had to give it up because of a head injury.

In the weeks that followed, we met as often as possible, walking in the public gardens or hiking in the veldt. Earthy and quiet, he loved nature and animals. From him, I learned what plants prospered in high altitudes and how to spot a poisonous snake. We spent time at a lodge near the Matopas, and back in Salisbury we went to drive-in movies, eating ice cream by starlight in the local park.

He worked for a tobacco company and had come north to escape South African Apartheid. Although he was of Irish descent some decades back, to me he seemed exotic enough to have come from another planet.

Sexual adventures in those days were fraught with problems. There were many complexities in our relationship – distance from Europe, political changes in Rhodesia, and his former divorce.

But he was considerate and kind and soon proposed marriage. I was not ready. Breaking up was inevitable, though heart-breaking and sad. Everyone has a secret, and this remains mine, a cherished memory of another time in a far-off land.

❧•☙

To assuage my grief over the break-up, I plunged myself into my work. I'd been given a house to design, and a bonus. I felt good about it.

I also bought myself a car. An old, slightly beaten-up Ford was all I could manage. Even so, it allowed me to have more freedom and to visit friends outside the city. But before I was able to make use of it, I needed a driver's licence.

I also needed a better place to live.

My first abode on Mrs Kelly's screened porch with its creeping vines and exotic plants was fun for a while, but the lack of privacy and my landlady's constant screaming at her drunken husband told me it was time to go.

❧•☙

Thankfully, the issue of the driver's licence and my living situation were both solved in one easy interaction.

At the local motor vehicles department, a pretty young English girl passed me the necessary papers. As I filled in the forms, she seemed eager to chat.

"I've just rented a small house in the Avenues and need a roommate. Would you be interested?"

When I nodded my head, she smiled. I went home and began to pack.

❖❖

Susan Emslie was tall and glamorous with beautiful brown eyes – an English version of Sophia Loren. She was funny and generous, but she was also divorced and unhappy. Her ambition was to marry, have lots of children, and live happily ever after. Sadly, she seemed to attract the wrong sort of men. Her former husband, a government scuba diver, was rarely around. They'd had an amicable divorce.

Susan and I developed a lifelong friendship. Years later, I met her parents, Henry and Dorothy, who were then retired and living in South Kensington. Her only sister worked for the BBC.

We complemented each other, sharing boyfriends, cars and adventures.

❖❖

With these changes, my life turned a corner. Our house on Baynes Avenue attracted members of the younger set. Beer and gin flowed freely. Sue loved to cook, and she attracted men like flies.

I made new friends: Martin Brown, an attractive young Englishman I designed a house for, and George Birch, a former Oxford scholar whom I suspected was a spy.

Mostly, our friends were running away from war-torn Europe or South Africa's Apartheid problems. We discussed books, local politics, and the winds of change sweeping the colony. Where would we go next? What could we do about the world?

I'd become used to the high altitude after enough time and took up tennis again. I was also spending more time in the office.

❖•❖

Having a telephone helped communication with my family. One day an unexpected call came from one of my McArevey cousins, Margo Bell, that changed my routine. She and her family had immigrated to Broken Hill in Northern Rhodesia, then part of Nyasaland, after World War II. We had written back and forth since my arrival in Salisbury, though I'd never visited.

"Hello," she said, "some good news from this end. Valerie is engaged to Eric Walsh, a young Anglo-Irish chap she met while she was staying here last year."

Valerie was the youngest of my McArevey cousins from Northern Ireland.

"Right now, she's in Ireland, staying with Mum and Dad in Dublin and looking for a wedding dress. She wants you to be her bridesmaid."

I didn't answer directly but said I would call back. There was much to consider about visiting: my absence from work, how I would get to Broken Hill from Salisbury, and so on.

Sue came to my rescue. "Why don't we both drive north together and spend a night at the Victoria Falls before going to Broken Hill?"

I could feel her enthusiasm.

"Let's use my car," she laughed. "Your old jalopy could never make it."

❈

Nick and Peter gave me time off from the office. Sue's car, a flashy red MG, looked in good shape. I was excited, gathered my stuff together, bought a suitable sunhat, and off we went.

More practical than I was, Sue packed sandwiches, water in an ice-filled container, and maps. As we stuffed our things into the ample boot, Sue remembered something and returned to the house.

"I'm frightened of guns," she said. "We should be protected, but with all the political unrest, let's take this just in case." She gleefully brandished a strange-looking weapon, something between a cricket bat and a police baton.

Driving on the one-lane dirt roads of the colony challenged our patience. Just keeping the tyres on the asphalt strip drove us crazy, but we laughed our way through it. People waved as the MG weaved through the congested shanty towns outside the city. I was concerned that the car's bright colour might attract too much attention.

The morning was still cool as we drove through open farmland. Small scantily-clad African people, mostly from the Bantu tribes, sold flowers and trinkets on the roadside. At one point, I spotted a tall Masai warrior with a loincloth and shield. The Masai were not common in this part of Africa.

"No stopping. This trip is going to take longer than you think," said Sue wisely. "We must make the Falls before dark."

She had a better sense of distance and map reading than I did.

As we continued, stately giraffes, ostriches and zebras were faintly visible against the banks of roadside trees. At midday, while the sun blazed above, we stopped briefly, raising the roof to keep cool and eat our sandwiches.

I happened to check the petrol gauge. It was almost empty. I'd forgotten about the petrol consumption of fancy cars and – worse still – we'd forgotten the spare can. I pointed this out to Sue.

"The map only shows one petrol station between here and the Falls," she said. "I'm leery of forging ahead. Let's wait and look for help."

Before long, a heavy truck with a cargo of caged goats lumbered towards us. I got out and waved. The driver, a large heavy-set White man in work clothes and a beaten-up bush hat, grudgingly refilled the petrol tank.

"The next station is about 26 miles up the road. You would never have made it," he pronounced. "It's not safe for young ladies like you to be driving alone along this lonely road."

He shook his head as he returned to his truck. I could hear the goats bleating as he left.

Relieved to have adequate petrol, we picked up speed, focusing on reaching the Falls before dark. It was now 4pm, which left us only forty-five minutes to get to our destination. We fell into silence. A barren veldt replaced the tree line bordering the highway. Traffic disappeared as we stared at the rapidly setting sun. Sue was driving when, out of nowhere, white puffs of what we believed to be smoke spiralled above the skyline.

"No, it's not smoke!" I cried with delight. "Just a reflection of water from the Falls."

❖•❖

The National Parks in Rhodesia closed at sundown. We just made it. Sue had made reservations at the hostel, which consisted of a group of rondavels encircling a beaten-up statue of Cecil Rhodes. I shivered in my cotton dress. A pungent loamy smell wafted from our little hut. A small wood-burning stove allowed us to heat water for tea. We slept soundly on narrow cots. I woke early to the sound of a clanging bell reminiscent of boarding school.

"I'm starving and need to pee," said Sue, struggling into her clothes.

A weathered concrete structure provided hot showers; the primitive toilet facilities smelled of Lysol. A few visitors joined us for a hearty breakfast of eggs, dark bread, and local sausage. We gathered our bags from the hut and headed for the Falls.

Few people showed up for the tour given by a burly park ranger. We followed him down a steep path into the rain forest. The air felt damp and moist, but not cold. My skin tingled; my hair hung limp and straight. The exotic smells, absence of bird life, and the roar of the Falls all seemed strange and spooky. After a long hike through clammy leaves, we started uphill towards the light.

In those days, the best way to see the Falls was from a rickety suspension bridge above the river. Terrified of heights, my stomach dropped. *Will I ever make it?*

Sue and other members of the group strode forward happily. I took a deep breath, grabbed the shaking handrails, looked straight ahead, and somehow finally reached the other side. In truth, I never saw the Falls to their full advantage.

"You look white as a sheet," said Sue when we finished the tour. "We should find some lunch and get on with the journey."

❖

A local concession stand outside the park provided Club Orange, salt crackers, and some biltong to chew. With few other cars on the road, we arrived in Broken Hill before dark. The Bell kids clapped as we swirled into the driveway of their house, a low-slung bungalow with an open screened-in porch. The youngest of the Bell children, five year old Belinda, told me years later how impressed she was with our arrival in that sporty red car.

Margo waved from the porch. Her husband Johnny, a dentist, was still at the office. I was curious to meet him.

Sue asked if she could play with the children. I had not seen Margo since she'd stayed with us at Fitzwilliam Place during World War II. Slim and petite, she resembled her mother, my Aunt Marjorie, more than her sisters did.

We caught up quickly, gossiping about the goings-on in the family. I was amused to see some pieces of fine furniture reminiscent of Courtney Hill House dotted around the spacious living room. I learned that Uncle Harry had sent them in one of my grandfather's old furniture crates.

"Tell me about Eric! Where did Valerie meet him?"

"They met at Mass in Livingstone. Johnny had a locum there. We had a short-term rental and took Val along with us. Eric was staying with his parents who had retired in the area."

"Daddy's home!" young Belinda shouted, running into the room. Johnny Bell, a tall attractive Englishman, greeted me with a smile. We talked of London and the war years, local politics, and stability in the colonies.

After dinner, we relaxed with sundowners on the screened-in porch. With the wedding only two months away, there was much to talk about. How many of the family were coming? Where would I find a suitable bridesmaid's dress?

❧

Once back at work in Salisbury in my normal routine, those two months slipped quickly by. The streets looked colourless and dull, the weather was hot and dry. With less than a few weeks until Valerie's wedding, I decided to make my own dress, as I had been unable to find one that I liked at the local shops.

I'd learnt to enjoy sewing during and after the war. Finding the fabric was easy, and white seemed the best choice. A Vogue pattern and Sue's electric sewing machine solved the problem. Excited and relaxed at the same time, I booked a flight to Lusaka with Rhodesian Airlines.

I arrived in Broken Hill in the early morning of the day before the wedding. Valerie greeted me on the front porch wearing a striped blue-and-white cotton dress and sandals. She looked slightly harried.

"We have a full house here and we're still looking for a place for us to stay tonight, on the night before the wedding. You must remember that old superstition," she said. "I'm sure something will turn up. You can just leave your bag in my room."

Fortunately, a family friend lent us a bedroom in his house nearby. The bed was small and uncomfortable. Valerie and I giggled and talked through the night without getting much sleep and woke up bleary-eyed but ready to face the day.

The small gothic revival Catholic church, set in a grove of flame trees, was almost full. At the reception afterwards at Johnny and Margo's house, I talked at length with Eric. Born to a military family living abroad in India, except for breaks at boarding schools in Ireland, he seemed more cosmopolitan than his contemporaries. His large extended Anglo-Irish family, a mixture of Protestants and Catholics, was open-minded and welcoming. He loved books and poetry and enjoyed writing. He was a perfect match for Valerie.

Margo and Johnny Bell gave a lovely reception at their house afterwards. I felt very much at home during the whole event.

❖•❖

The following day, I left Broken Hill with both joy and sadness, wondering how many of these wonderful people would cross my path again.

Once back in Salisbury, I found Susan unsettled and anxious. She'd had a falling out with her latest boyfriend.

Additionally, our living expenses had increased, and we'd needed a new roommate. The best candidate had been Keith Johnson who, unfortunately, was driving her crazy.

"Why don't you get a new job?" I suggested impatiently. "Or take up fencing?"

Things finally settled down when we both took up fencing, which was the newest craze in the colony. We were able to stretch out our leg muscles and laugh at the contorted poses we found ourselves in.

❖

But I also felt unsettled and unsure how long I wanted to remain in Rhodesia.

I told Sue I was going on an extended trip to South Africa and would consider leaving for home shortly after I returned.

Before leaving Africa, I did just that, taking a long trip from Mozambique to South Africa, where Apartheid was still a force to be reckoned with.

Groups of armed militia patrolled certain areas and enforced a curfew after dark. In Cape Town, I climbed Table Mountain and rejoiced in the view. But, despite the area's beauty, I knew it was not the place for me.

Returning to Salisbury, we packed our steamer trunks and said our goodbyes.

❖

Valerie and Eric lived in the Lukasa area where they raised three little boys while Eric worked for the government. In 1963, they immigrated to Perth in Western

Australia, where Eric and Val continue to live. Thanks to the internet, we keep in touch.

The next time I saw them was decades later, when I was married with two children and living in Montclair, New Jersey.

❧

Johnny, Margo, and their children returned to Westport in the west of Ireland, except for their eldest son Paul, who decided to stay and now works in South Africa. Sadly, Johnny, Margo, and Tom, one of their children, are all dead now. Little Belinda grew up to marry Hugh McCullagh, a professor of geology at University College Dublin, and has four children. She and her family continue to live in Dublin close to my sister Esmay.

❧

Susan took a new job and later met a lovely down-to-earth Englishman, Peter Trumble. She became the model housewife with five children she'd always aspired to be.

We kept up over the years. My husband Don Price and I met up with the Trumbles during one of our visits to London. She died a few years after that.

❧

As for me, I found a job with an architectural firm in Bloomsbury that specialised in high-end restaurants. I watched the world go by, eating lunch on the steps of the British Museum. My bedsitter, close to the London Underground, shook every time a train went by, but it was warm and full of sunshine. What happened next is another story.

❧·❧

Northern Rhodesia became the Republic of Zambia in 1964 in a seamless, swift transition. Southern Rhodesia did not become the Republic of Zimbabwe until 1980. Because of two African-backed aligned revolutions, the British held off until then to prevent violence and bloodshed.

Left to right: Eleanor, Eric Walsh, Valerie Walsh, John Bermingham, Belinda Bell, and Moira Walsh.

PICKING UP THREADS,
AND AN AMERICAN ADVENTURE

When my mother suggested I buy a trunk, she must have known I would never return to Ireland, at least not on a permanent basis. She must have thought about my trips back and forth from London and Southern Rhodesia and been tired of my wanderings, though she never commented.

A widow for seven years by the time I returned, she lived with Aunty Daisy and my youngest sister Esmay. My two other sisters, Ann and Mary Rose, had both married.

Protected by her sister Daisy and surrounded by friends and family, my mother seemed preoccupied and comfortable.

❧

Leaving for America felt both similar to and different from my previous trips. It was easy to say goodbye to the family but difficult, as it had always been, to leave Ireland.

My sister Ann and cousin Lorna accompanied me to Southampton, where the boat was to leave from. I don't remember much about the trip, except that the crossing was rough. I was seasick most of the time, and my cabin mate talked incessantly and smoked in bed.

The impact of entering New York Harbour for the first time was breathtaking. Lights twinkled in tall buildings, and the sky was streaked with red. Sirens blared as we approached the dock. Beneath the excitement, I was apprehensive and hoped I would find my cousin Roddy McCaffrey, who had promised to meet me.

Like me, Roddy was a graduate architect of Ireland's national university and had been working in Manhattan for almost two years. We met without much trouble. He looked the same but more confident than I remembered and wore a well-cut lightweight cotton suit.

"Let's go to my apartment and have a drink. I've booked a room for you at the YWCA," he told me after we'd said proper hellos. "It will be more comfortable than the hard floor at my place."

It took a long time to find a cab – lots of pushing and shoving. The driver spoke accented English and drove fast, dodging and weaving through the traffic. Horns blared and lights flashed. I sat on the edge of my seat. Roddy laughed and told me to relax.

"This is Manhattan. Everything moves fast. These guys know their way even if it seems like they don't speak English to you," he said.

In less than ten minutes we were carrying my overstuffed suitcase up four flights of narrow stairs that smelled of Clorox and stale cabbage. The apartment on the fourth floor was fresh and airy, a large sub-divided space with scant furnishings, some familiar reproductions of contemporary artists and a faded Kilim rug on the parquet floor. Accustomed to the cold unheated houses back in Ireland, I felt hot and uncomfortable. Roddy opened the window.

"It's impossible to control the heat," he laughed.

I didn't realise at the time that, four years later, I would be living in the exact same space and opening the same window, but that's another story.

❧•❧

We ate at a small restaurant two blocks away. The tables were squished together, the napkins were snowy white, and the waiter spoke with yet another foreign accent. People talked in hushed tones. Roddy told me about his work and expressed his excitement over living in Manhattan.

He had organised a trip to Philadelphia on the weekend to see a new building by the architect Louis Kahn and hoped I would come with him. Though I only had a week before flying to California and wanted to explore New York, I agreed to the offer.

He reminded me I should phone Yvonne Westfried, a family friend who had sponsored me to enter the United States.

"She's a charming lady and has already asked me to dinner. I think you'll like her."

Though curious about meeting Yvonne, I was bone tired. The call would have to wait.

❧•❧

The YWCA on the Lower East Side faced a busy thoroughfare. My room was small and sparsely furnished. Lights twinkled through the window. Too tired to sleep, I felt alone and nervous. *How will I find my way around this vast metropolis? Have I bitten off more than I can chew?*

Street noises intruded – the blaring wail of an ambulance tore through the streets. Even the building shook. I realised later that the YWCA was close to a subway stop. Eventually, I drifted off to sleep.

❖

A strident bell got me out of bed the next day. The previous night's anxiety had vanished. I was ready to find breakfast and a telephone.

It was mild and breezy outside. The street was already bustling with people. No one paid attention to the traffic lights, but it didn't matter. The traffic was congested and slow. A nearby coffee shop looked inviting, and I was ready to eat.

The place was small and crowded, with a counter and chrome-plated stools like the drug stores I'd read about; it smelled of pickles and baking. I grabbed a menu. The man next to me was eating a round bun with a hole in the centre and drinking soda; someone else ordered eggs-over-easy. I ordered the scrambled eggs and black coffee. It seemed safe. Roddy had warned me never to ask for tea.

I was alone and excited. The man perched next to me must have sensed I wasn't a local.

"You should try a bagel with lox and cream cheese," he said, pointing to the bun he was eating with a hole in the centre.

I thanked him for telling me about bagels but decided to stick to my scrambled eggs.

Fortunately, there was also a telephone in the coffee shop. In those days, there were telephones on almost every street corner. My first task was to call Yvonne and arrange a meeting.

❧•❧

Yvonne Westfried was something of a legend in the family. She had attended a Sacred Heart convent in Paris with my father's sister Clare. Daddy had spent holidays with the Westfried family when he was a graduate student in Vienna and later visited their Paris apartment with my mother.

The daughter of an English father and an Irish mother, Yvonne had spent most of her life in France. Just before the occupation of Paris during World War II, Yvonne, her Jewish husband Ernest, and their son Alex had come to America. Their daughter Arlette, who had remained in Paris, had died under mysterious circumstances.

❧•❧

I dialled nervously, not knowing what to expect. Would Yvonne be as nice to me as she was to my father, or was she now too old to bother?

"You *must* come to lunch. I want to hear *all* about the family," she said in a clear, bird-like voice, before giving me directions to her apartment.

Park Avenue and 86th Street was a long way from where I was, but I had time to spare and decided to walk.

The subway could wait, and figuring out which bus to take was too much trouble.

The day had warmed up, and the rush hour crowds dispersed as I zigzagged along the cavernous streets. Delivery trucks completely blocked the cross streets, smelling of gas fumes and garbage. Drivers shouted and honked their horns; tired men pushed trolleys into warehouses. The tall buildings seemed to close in, blocking the sky.

I could tell from the small shops along the streets that I was in a seedy area. There were few pedestrians around, and all the trucks had suddenly disappeared. The place seemed dark and sinister. With the help of a map, I found my way to a busy street, which turned out to be Fifth Avenue. Though nothing happened to me, the experience was a signal to be careful.

I was fascinated by the buildings and the different faces within the passing crowd. My neck strained from looking at the gardens above me and intricate rooftop details; I lost track of time. It was almost noon, and my feet ached from the long walk. In desperation, I hailed a cab.

❖

The Westfrieds lived in a 1930s-style apartment block with horizontal ribbon windows. A formidable doorman in liveried uniform guarded the entrance. He looked me up and down, and then said he needed to make a call. The foyer had too many mirrors and an oversized container of fake flowers.

A slight elderly gentleman with a waxed moustache came to the apartment door. His beautifully tailored suit had a European flair, and he wore white spats.

"I'm Ernest Westfried," he said. "You must be Eleanor, our young Irish friend. I remember your father well."

He kissed my hand formally and led me to a large L-shaped room over-furnished with French and East Asian antiques. It smelled of perfume and beeswax. Heavily embossed plates and family portraits graced the walls, and a red lacquered screen divided the dining area from the living space – an old-fashioned room in a modern building.

A diminutive woman in a flowery silk dress emerged from a room off the hallway and enveloped me in a warm embrace.

"Ma petite Eleanor. *Comment ça va?* You are so like your mother," she said, changing to English.

I could see something of the former beauty my father had described, the pointed nose and striking blue eyes, the auburn hair streaked with grey – a truly French face, reminiscent of the writer Colette.

While Ernest served spritzers, Yvonne talked about my father and his visits to her farm in Czechoslovakia and later in Paris. Lunch was a chicken dish with mushrooms served by a sad-looking maid in a black dress.

She had a foreign voice, but it wasn't French – yet another accent. Yvonne told me later she was a refugee from Bulgaria.

WEST TO A NEW HORIZON

The seatbelt sign came on, and I awoke with a start. The plane lurched sideways and seemed as though it would fall out of the sky. I shivered, pulling a light jacket around my shoulders.

I was freezing after a week of sight-seeing in warm Manhattan with my cousin Roddy.

"We are approaching the Bay Area and should land in ten minutes," a strident voice announced through the public address system.

Now, I was very much awake and trying to collect my thoughts. *What happens if no one's waiting for me at the airport?*

My crazy impulses had landed me in trouble before, but this was serious business. Had I crossed an ocean, as well as the North American continent, on a whim?

❖

I'd met Patricia and Michael Graham in London the previous March at my cousin Nuala's house on Cheyne Walk in Chelsea. I remember daffodils in the small garden, air smelling of lilac and spring, and drinking champagne with them on the flagstone patio.

The Grahams were open and friendly. We talked about the new house they had just built in Tiburon outside San Francisco. Then, they had asked me to visit. I hardly knew them, but it didn't seem to matter. My cousin in London assured me that the invitation was genuine. I was in a bleak mood at the time, working at a dead-end job and brooding over an unsuitable romance. Why not accept? I had often thought about going to the United States, and here was the perfect opportunity!

Michael Graham, a fighter pilot during the war, was ruggedly handsome. I knew that he had been in love with my cousin Nuala. Though she rejected him for another, they remained friends. After the war, Michael went to America, finally settling in San Francisco. Somewhere along the way, he met and married Patricia Whaley, a glamorous redhead from West Virginia. Whenever they came to London, Nuala entertained them.

By the time my recollections had passed me by, the airport was shrouded in mist. A fellow passenger told me it was typical for this time of year. Feeling chilled in my thin cotton dress, I knew my clothes were all wrong. In New York, they'd been too hot; here, it was the other way round.

After getting off the plane, I started searching for the Grahams' phone number in my bag and began wondering about public transportation. This airport was miles from San Francisco. I scanned the crowd, considered going to the information booth, and eventually decided against it.

How long should I wait? Almost an hour had passed since we landed. *Where are they?*

Then, suddenly, I spotted them through the crowd, waving madly as they approached. Pat was wearing a denim skirt, a beige twinset and pearls, while Michael was looking very British in his blazer and flannels. Pat gave me a big hug.

"How lovely to see you," she said in her lilting Southern voice. "Our friends are always quick to accept our invitations, but they don't usually follow through."

❧

On the way to their house, Michael did most of the talking, describing the scenery and commenting on the traffic as we drove up the Peninsula past Daly City into San Francisco.

"It's misty until we cross the bridge. We live on the other side of the Golden Gate Bridge, in Tiburon, which gets more sunshine," he rattled off.

The Grahams' house at Pelican Point in Tiburon was built into a slope above the water. The rooms spread out from an octagonal deck that cantilevered above. The day was sunny but cool; the air smelled of pine bark.

"We love to cook outdoors, even in winter," Pat told me.

Totally exhausted by the journey, I barely heard her, but I do have a vague memory of Michael grilling lamb chops and offering white wine. I don't recall much after the night closed in, except the need to sleep.

❧

Life on Pelican Point was tightly organised. Residents, mostly married without children, rose early, drove to work, and returned in the evening. After a few days of this, the magic faded. I was used to the city and felt trapped without public transportation. The roads had no sidewalks and walking anywhere was impossible. I caught glimpses of the Golden Gate Bridge through the morning mist, but otherwise, San Francisco seemed miles away.

Understanding my situation, Pat and Michael suggested that I accompany Michael on his way to work in the city, which would give me a chance to look for a job and explore.

❧•❧

I loved the city with its mists, smells, steep hills and unexpected vistas, the clanging cable cars, and elegant stores. But looking for work was a challenge. The architects I called on were not at all receptive to women. Some even suggested I try the typing pool. I felt angry, but remained confident that things would work out in my favour.

One night sometime later, the Grahams invited me to join them at a neighbourhood party the upcoming weekend. It was a posh black-tie affair honouring a group of Hungarian fencers who had escaped from the Soviet Union. I was excited at the idea of dressing up and meeting people, though uncertain about the Hungarian fencers.

The host, a journalist, was doing a story on the fencers, and the people at the party seemed to know each other. Michael introduced me to a tall man with a craggy face called Tex, who worked for a sports magazine. He was funny, sexy, and didn't seem to mind that I knew nothing about baseball. We drank Scotch and ate sushi on the deck.

"I need to interview the fencers and must find my interpreter," Tex said. "Please don't leave before I return."

I hoped the Grahams were having such a good time they wouldn't want to leave too early.

Apart from the fencers and Tex, there weren't any single people around. I was peering down at the water musing about him when a small voice interrupted my thoughts.

"Are you the Irish girl who's staying with the Grahams?" It was a young woman; she was small and waif-like with hazel eyes, short black hair, and a round freckled face

"I'm Barbara, and I work for the host. We must be the only single people here, except for the Hungarians and that handsome guy you were talking to," she said with an impish grin.

Call it instant friendship. The connection seemed to be mutual. We talked about everything, including her family in Philadelphia and mine in Ireland.

"You must come into the city. I share an apartment on Child Street near Telegraph Hill. Let's meet next week, and I'll help you find somewhere to live," she said.

By this time, Tex had returned and was full of stories about the Hungarians.

Dependent on a ride back to the city, Barbara left early. The party was breaking up. Tex dropped me at Pelican Point and kissed my cheek. I wasn't upset that he never called after that night. It was a beautiful memory – and now I had other plans.

THE HEADY YEARS IN SAN FRANCISCO

I'd only been staying with Pat and Michael in Tiberon for a few days when I realised I needed to move into the city, meet younger people, and look for a job. Meeting Barbara Hippel at the party given for the Hungarian fencers only reinforced this realisation. I decided to take her up on her offer to meet for lunch in the city.

❧

Sunshine played on the water below the cantilevered deck, and I felt excited and eager to meet up with Barbara. We'd already talked on the phone and arranged a time and place.

"Let's get going," Michael said. He was kindly giving me a ride on his way to work in Vallejo on the other side of the Bay.

He glanced at the light cotton dress I was wearing. "Remember to bring a sweater."

The city was shrouded in mist and barely visible that morning, and the Bridge seemed to go on forever. The air smelled of ozone and diesel. Soft clouds drifted gently

137

through the pylons; a few sailboats clung to the coast. The traffic was moving fast, but this didn't seem to bother Michael, who was eager to talk and give advice.

"I can see from the address that your friend lives in North Beach. Originally that was an Italian neighbourhood. Old men still play Bocci in Washington. But now, it's also the centre of the Beat Generation, which started in the early fifties," he rattled off. "Tourists and locals flock there in the evenings. You must go! It can be lots of fun."

◆◆◆

By the time we reached North Beach, the air had become cold and damp. I began to be glad for the cardigan.

Michael assured me the sun would break through as he dropped me off outside Barbara's apartment on Child Street with the final parting words, "I'll pick you up here on my way home."

Barbara opened the door to her apartment and greeted me with a big hug; she was wearing a black, close-fitting outfit, and her short, tightly cut hair was spiked with green.

"I'm delighted you've come. Here, meet my friends Maureen Murphy and her husband Murph. They live in the apartment upstairs," she said, pointing towards the young couple with her.

They were both casually dressed in cut-offs and T-shirts. Suddenly, I felt decidedly out of place in my fashionable New York dress.

"Nice to meet someone who's *really 'Irish'*," said Maureen. "We're both teachers who moved here recently from

Boston. We were weary of the conformity and miserable weather and decided we needed a change. It's easy to get work in this city, provided you have a degree and some experience."

"I'm also in the job market," I told them, adding that I had a degree in architecture. I also mentioned that I needed to find an apartment, preferably in this neighbourhood.

"Yes, this is the place to be," Murph said. "You'll find a diverse mix of young professionals, mostly from Europe and other parts of the United States."

After Maureen and her husband wished me luck and returned upstairs to their apartment, Barbara made more coffee. We slouched on a beaten-up sofa in the corner of the sparsely furnished room. Despite the booming foghorn, bright sunlight streamed in through the windows. I tossed off my cardigan.

"I love your dress," said Barbara. "You could easily wear that to the office. It's still formal dress here for office work, though I believe women in Europe already wear casual pants."

I nodded, glad to know I would have some appropriate clothes for my job hunt. I learned that Barbara came from a well-to-do conservative family in Philadelphia – her father was a lawyer. She herself had a degree in liberal arts from Mount Holyoke, a well-known women's college in Massachusetts.

"You'll meet lots of young professional men in the Bay Area, though not always ones you would like to marry," she said, with a wistful far-away look. "It's a friendly place, very different from the East Coast."

I asked her about the City Lights Bookstore and other Beat hangouts.

"I often go there," Barbara replied. "You never know who you could run into. Jazz clubs like the Hungry I are fun but quite expensive, but there are also other places. If you would like, we could wander over this evening. Why don't you call Michael and tell him you'll be staying here overnight and checking out the Beats? I'll catch up on some office work while you grab a nap."

A few hours later, when we were ready to leave, Barbara told me that a friend, Jean-Paul Sablon, would meet us at Louie's, a small café close to Washington Square.

"He's an architect from Lyon. Perhaps he might have some advice about finding a job," she said.

It was already twilight by the time we arrived at Louie's. Jean-Paul, a skinny young man with straggly black hair and friendly eyes, was already there, exuding energy.

"I know several of your countrymen, all architects," he said, kissing me on both cheeks. "I've also run into others from London. But enough about work. Now for some local colour. I believe Alan Ginsberg may be at City Lights this evening."

Laughter and music floated through the crowded streets as we made our way up the hill to Broadway.

"What is that strange smell?" I asked Barbara, as we passed Grant Avenue.

She laughed as she initiated me. "That's cannabis or pot! Do you fancy a joint? It's freely available. Lots of my friends like it, but I prefer the local red wine."

How naïve can you get? I scolded myself. *I'll have to try some …*

I noticed a large storefront window on the other side of the street displaying brightly dressed transvestites on swings. They smiled and waved to the crowd.

Barbara shook her head. "In most other states this would be illegal. At least here they are being noticed."

We had good luck at City Lights Bookstore. Though Ginsberg had cancelled his engagement, another poet recited his *Howl*. I bought a copy of Jack Kerouac's *On the Road*. Afterwards, Jean-Paul suggested we go to Luigi's for dinner.

According to Barbara, Luigi's was one of several restaurants that were popular with young people, especially those from Europe.

"They serve a single course with lots of good bread and local wine. It's an easy and inexpensive way to meet new friends," she said.

As Barbara and I queued to get into the restaurant, Jean-Paul was already ahead of us, chatting with a young couple.

"I just invited my friends from London, John and Val Winters, to sit opposite us," he said, walking back to queue with us. "John works in my office, and Val is a social worker."

We were soon ushered inside.

❧•❧

Red-and-white checked cloths covered the long table. Brightly coloured posters were scattered along the white walls of the open space. The air smelled of basil and garlic. We started to relax as we helped ourselves to a steaming stew.

Understated John Winters, a tall, sandy-haired man wearing an open shirt and khakis, turned out to be friendly.

"I'm a representative of the Royal Institute of British Architects, here on sabbatical," he said. "We had to get out of London. The lack of jobs, poor food, and general dreariness was depressing.

"Finding a job should be easy for you," he continued, turning to me. "I've met several architects from Ireland, some you probably know. The offices are small compared to London, but the people are always interested in what's going on overseas."

"The climate in this part of the city often reminds me of home, but you just have to cross the Bridge to find sunshine," said Valerie, a blue-eyed blonde. "I am sure you also won't have trouble getting a place to live. We have a large apartment on Sonoma Street, not far from Barbara's place."

❧•❧

By the time we'd discussed everything from Bauhaus architecture to Civil Rights and the Vietnam War, Luigi's Restaurant was about to close.

"Please drop by our apartment," said Val, giving me her address and phone number. "We'd like to know how you're getting on."

❧•❧

Back at Barbara's apartment on Child Street, before we collapsed into our beds, she handed me a key to her apartment and a map of North Beach.

"I'll be at work by the time you get up. It might be interesting for you to explore the neighbourhood. I'll leave cereal and a teapot in the kitchen. On a student visit to Northern Ireland after the war, I discovered tea with milk, and it's now my favourite drink for breakfast."

❖

I slept in late the next day, and it was almost midday when I ventured outside. The mist had cleared off, and sunshine was streaming through fat white clouds. A large cruise ship entered the Bay.

Except for a scattering of older folks, the streets on Telegraph Hill were empty and quiet. As I traversed the labyrinth of narrow streets, a pleasant breeze whipped through my unruly hair. The map let me know the part of the area I was in bordered Chinatown. The smell of unknown spices wafted through the air. I spied a FOR RENT sign on the side of an arched opening and decided to check it out, darting through the arch up a spiral stairway.

A young, bearded man wearing a tie-dyed tunic was waiting to beckon me into what must have been his office.

"My name is Craig. I'm an art student", he said with a faint smile. "My family owns this building and lives on the first floor. The apartment for rent is on the second, and it's a single-tenant occupancy. I hope that won't bother you. It may be small, but everything is built in."

I observed that the cooking facilities were modest, but the shower and toilet facilities were contemporary. None of that really mattered, as I had instantly fallen in love with the breath-taking view of the city.

❖

I moved into #5 Reno Place a week later. My only luggage was the two steamer trunks I had sent ahead of time, which were waiting to be picked up at the San Francisco docks. Barbara and her friends picked up the trunks and other bits and pieces for me.

Michael Graham was sceptical and amused at the prospect.

"This will be a short rental, but it looks like lots of fun," he laughed. "If I were young again, I'd move right in."

Now, with an address and a telephone number, it was time to look for a job.

ARCHITECTURE, AND THE CHALLENGES OF A NEW JOB

Finding work in San Francisco was problematic when women architects were still a novelty. Having checked the list of offices Michael had given me and after being questioned at one firm about my typing skills, I felt it was time to regroup.

Adrian Gail, a young English architect I had met at John and Val Winter's place came to my rescue. Both being transplants from war-torn London with mutual friends here and in New York, Adrian and I had lots in common.

"Call this number to ask for an appointment," he told me. "It's a small architect's office on the campus of UC Medical Centre on Golden Gate Heights. The location seems a little incongruous, but there is lots of building going on there."

❧•❧

A few days later, I was in a streetcar heading across the city to Golden Gate Heights. By the time I reached my destination, the sky had darkened. I shivered in my light linen dress and grabbed a cardigan from my loose carrier bag. Outside, the air smelled cold and damp. The huge hospital, a faceless multi-storey structure, loomed high above the street.

I braced myself. *Now to find the Architect's Office building.*

A sign told me to follow a flight of stone steps up the hill and turn right at the top. Set in a grove of trees, the small-framed one-storey structure with its yellow door seemed straight from another century. A pleasant middle-aged receptionist with a nice smile greeted me warmly.

"You must be Eleanor Price. My name is Agnes. Mr Wagstaff and Mr Grenfell will be with you shortly," she said, showing me into a large brightly painted room with a view of the Pacific Ocean on one side and a plethora of architectural sketches and drawings on the other.

The scene took me back to Southern Rhodesia and my days with Montgomery & Oldfield.

Jack Wagstaff entered. He was a tall, elegant man, slightly grey at the temples, wearing a tweed jacket and a formal shirt and tie. He extended his welcome with a strong handshake.

Shorter in stature and younger looking, his partner, Dick Grenfell, had an easy smile and a relaxed manner. I noticed he was wearing cords and an open shirt.

All business, Jack proceeded to explain the division of work.

"Dick supervises the designs of plans presented by the doctors, and I'm the construction manager of the campus buildings. You will be a liaison between the doctors and outside architects. Success is all about communication. I hope you are a good listener," he said. "You may often be asked to make sketches. Some of the doctors know little about building and become impatient with the architects. The job is yours to make of it as you will.

"Right now, I'm off to a meeting," he finished, standing up. "But don't hesitate to ask Dick about other aspects of working for a hospital complex."

He strode out, leaving me alone with Dick.

"I hope you're a morning person," Dick said. "We start at eight but close promptly at 4:30pm. It's an early start, but you will always find a seat on the earlier tram."

Dick seemed eager to chat, telling me more about the neighbourhood than the work I might have to do.

"Remember to always bring a cardigan or wrap. It rarely warms up on the Heights. If you like to play tennis, you'll find public courts near the streetcar stop," he said, giving me a rough map. "My family uses them from time to time, but they are rarely crowded. There's a Russian bistro nearby that has tasty borsch and blinis."

I thanked him for the information and agreed to start the following day. So far, the atmosphere there was friendly and very different from the large impersonal offices in London.

❧❧

On my return from Golden Gate Heights, I wondered about hidden aspects of my new job. Would I need a car to visit architects in other parts of the city or maybe to cross the Bay Bridge to Berkeley?

Back at Reno Place, the mail brought two unexpected letters demanding my attention. One was from Mummy's old school chum, Dr Clare Malone, and the other was from my Irish friend Mary King.

My impression of the first letter was that the doctor sounded bossy and imperious, so I decided I had better call her immediately. Contrary to my initial impression, Dr Clare turned out to sound friendly and pleased when I reached her on the phone.

"Robin and I will be in San Francisco in a few weeks and would love you to dine with us," she said, referring to her husband Robin Schweiger. "I haven't met anyone who knows about my family for years. We'll contact you a few days beforehand."

The other letter, from my friend Mary, was brief and to the point but made me realise I needed to spring into action quickly.

She wrote:

> My visa finally came through, so I plan to arrive in two weeks. I have your phone number and address – will take a taxi to your apt.

Mary was coming to me? To stay in Reno Place?

However scenic the view, Reno Place was only suitable for one person. I needed to hurry and find a bigger apartment!

❧✦❧

At dinner later with Val, John and Adrian, I asked them to check rentals in the neighbourhood.

Luck plays funny tricks. During the following week, I returned from work one afternoon to find my apartment completely ransacked.

The landlord promised to increase security and forego payment for the next month. Of course, these measures could not make up for the loss of Mummy's emerald ring and a beautiful evening gown, but I had no time for recriminations. Mary's arrival meant I had to organise and move on.

❧✦❧

A large apartment on the third floor of John and Val's building on Sonoma Street became available at the last minute, and I moved in the day after I viewed it.

Visiting the local thrift shops and with the help of friends, I furnished the place quickly, luckily finding two mattresses and some sheets without having to spend too much money. The previous tenant had left behind a chest of drawers and a few odd chairs. Michael Graham's wife Pat dropped by with a selection of things for the kitchen.

Fortunately, Mary was not fastidious, something I remembered from camping trips in our childhood.

❧✦❧

Work at the medical centre was a new experience, from finding my way around the vast hospital to finding somewhere to eat. The first day, I took along a sandwich, which I ate in my small office.

One day, Dick knocked on my door and asked me to lunch.

"You should really make use of the hospital dining room. The food there is excellent and cheap," he said, as we trudged up the steep hill. "You just have to understand the system."

A sharp wind blowing in from the ocean reminded me that I needed to buy a winter anorak.

The dining room was vast and crowded. We finally sat down to enjoy a well-balanced meal. He told me to expect a call from a doctor in the oncology department, where we'd heard there was a big surge in cancer research.

"Be sure to ask me if you have questions. Most of the doctors are reasonable, but you never know," Dick cautioned.

❖

Before long, I received a call from Dr Clare, asking me to dinner at the Fairmont Hotel on Nob Hill.

"It's very posh," said Adrian when I told him my plans. "I hope you have something more fashionable to wear than those scruffy cut-offs."

I quickly assured him, "Don't worry about me. Dressing up is very much a family thing. I could never let Mummy down."

I treated myself to a taxi that night. The Fairmont, an elaborate post-modern building, had a magnificent view of the city and waterfront. The doorman asked my name, then escorted me to a corner table in the huge dining room. Dr Clare, a middle-sized woman with weathered freckled skin and a wide smile, welcomed me with a hug.

"You are so like your mother, it's uncanny," she said. "It's marvellous to see somebody who knows Wexford. Now, you must meet my husband."

Robin Schweiger, a tall, fine-looking grey-haired man with a mild European accent, kissed me on both cheeks.

"I come from Switzerland, famed for watches and cuckoo clocks," he said with a chuckle. "Two years ago, when Clare retired, I decided to start an electronics company in Oregon."

"Portland, where we live, is cold and damp, almost worse than Ireland," Clare added. "But we have a vacation house on Lake Tahoe, with a large guest cottage. You and your friends are welcome to visit. We love having young people around."

Clare was interested in my job at the UC Hospital and commented on medical advances since the 1920s. I felt the desire to ask her more about my O'Keefe grandfather, but her memories would have to wait. Clare could sense my exhaustion after my workday and asked Robin to call me a taxi. After farewell hugs and kisses, I vanished into the chilly darkness.

❧•❧

A little while later, my friend Mary arrived, late in the afternoon as expected. Her shoulder-length blondish hair was slightly dishevelled from the long trip, but her green eyes were as lively as ever.

"It's wonderful to be here," she said, as we dragged her large suitcase up the stairs. "Dublin is dreary, with few professional jobs available. Living with Granny Burke and Uncle Paddy became confining and impossible. I didn't have enough money to move out on my own."

Mary's father, a doctor, worked in London, leaving his four children in the care of their grandmother in Dublin. Granny Burke lived on Mount Street close to Merrion Square, which had been built between 1763–1776 and was one of the finest examples of Georgian architecture – opening it up for public use had been one of my Aunty Daisy's projects. We had been friends since college days.

After a cup of tea and some shortbread biscuits, I showed Mary to the larger of the two bedrooms.

"I hope you don't mind a mattress on the floor for now, but we have loads of blankets, and the heating system works," I told her.

Later, we joined the gang at Val and John's for a communal dinner. I contributed a bottle of wine and a tuna casserole. Mary wore a slick black-and-white striped dress, relaxing easily with the group, who besieged her with questions.

Shortly after graduation, while I went to work in Africa, Mary had worked in Dublin and had come to know many of our former colleagues from UCD, who were now employed in the Bay Area.

Besides my friend Adrian, we were joined by Vincent O'Kelly, an engineer from Dublin. The party broke up around midnight.

Vinnie arranged to meet Mary for lunch the following day at Fisherman's Wharf.

A week or two after her arrival in San Francisco, Vinnie helped find Mary a job with a construction company. I was relieved about this, since Mary, who was an excellent draftswoman, had never finished her degree.

❧

Mary, the ultimate storyteller, was a great hit with our group. Together we met young American professionals, mostly lawyers, at our open table dinners on Telegraph Hill.

I recall a particular incident when a young lawyer and recent graduate of Stanford University, Fred, decided to remark, in his southern California drawl, "You speak excellent English for an Irish girl."

Mary replied caustically without missing a beat, "Have you ever heard of George Bernard Shaw?"

He shook his head, "No."

Ironically, those two became close friends. Another lawyer, Berney Marchant, who hailed from Chicago, and a Yale graduate, Jim Drumond, became part of our group. I discovered that most of these young men came from wealthy families, and thus could enjoy the leisure of finding themselves before facing the real world.

❧

It eventually dawned on me that weekend activities were such a big part of life in San Francisco that I really needed to buy a car.

Once again, my good friend and mentor Michael Graham came to my aid, finding an almost-new Chevrolet sedan for $200.00. Since both Mary and I had extensive driving experience, we both quickly passed the California driver's test.

It goes without saying, however, that driving on the opposite side of the street took a while to get used to ...

Eleanor (left) and Dr Clare in California.

LIFELONG FRIENDS

I was tired and hungover, my head ached, and I needed coffee. A flash of sunlight reminded me that it was morning. Mary staggered from the bathroom and slumped onto the beaten-up sofa.

"Too many parties, too many visitors, booze, pot, and late nights," she said. "We need to get out of the city."

I nodded and ran downstairs for the paper, threw it to her and started making coffee. *Where to go?* I asked myself. *Across the Bay Bridge to sunshine? Down south to Pebble Beach and Monterey? Or north to the Pacific beaches and Mount Tamalpais?*

"Listen to this," said Mary, looking up from the paper. "'*For rent: two-bedroom cottage with large living space and bathroom facilities on two acres of land facing sea, half a mile south of Bolinas Village. Owner on overseas assignment. Yearly rental $1,000 or monthly at $100*'. What do you think?"

"Let's go have a look! If nothing else, we'll see another part of the coast, get some fresh air, and maybe have a swim at one of the beaches," I replied, stuffing books, a heavy sweater, and nightwear into a duffle bag.

And so, off we went.

-≻•≺-

A misty fog hung over the city as we headed for the Golden Gate Bridge. Mary looked so happy as she manipulated the twists and turns of the coastal highway. The joy of driving a big car with a radio was still a novelty.

"I can't imagine how my small beaten-up Vauxhall would take this twisty road," she said.

The sun broke through as we arrived at the realtor's office in Bolinas Village. The realtor, a big man with a well-trimmed beard and a strong handshake, introduced himself as Henry McIntyre. We set off shortly after making our introductions.

"You were smart to call me early. The phone has rung off the hook since I arrived at the office. This cottage is a steal!" he said, as we drove along the dirt road.

Except for a few windswept trees, the terrain looked bare and untamed. The small building, more like a log cabin than a rustic cottage, seemed in good shape, but the spectacular view was enough to entice us to move in, regardless of what the inside looked like.

"An electric heating system is available at a modest cost. They also have a primitive barbeque pit," Henry said. "Why don't you check out everything before making a decision? I'll wait in the car."

We decided to rent the cottage for two months and go from there. Henry drove us back to his office where we signed the papers, and he handed over the keys.

"Remember to phone me if you have problems," he said. "I suggest you try our local restaurant. They have the best clam chowder."

Lightheaded and hungry, we took his advice. After a hearty BLT on sourdough bread and a bowl of chowder, Mary suddenly looked up.

"Are we crazy? I love the place, but every weekend for two months?" she said with a giggle.

"Absolutely not," I replied. "We can offer the cottage to our good friends in the city in exchange for their hospitality and help. Adrian, the Winters, and Barbara would love it. Let's stay in the cottage overnight and make sure everything works."

We bought milk, cereal, tea and essentials at the convenience store and headed back to the cottage. Sleeping in proper beds was a treat, and the heating system worked. I even found some camping equipment and toys for children.

❧•❧

The following day we headed for the beach. Despite the warm day, no one but Mary and I was swimming. Yes, the Pacific Ocean is cold, but it compares favourably with the Irish Sea.

We used the cottage with various friends for the next two weekends. Some of our visitors, especially those with children, loved going to the beach with its easy access, safe swimming, and volleyball. Others, including Mary and I, preferred hiking the many trails of Mount Tamalpais.

These weekend trips helped us to focus on problems at work and play. Life was changing on Sonoma Street. Another couple, Sandy Zane, his English wife, Judy Hunter Blair, and their baby Lucy moved into one of the upstairs apartments.

Married couples and children made use of our cottage camping equipment. To help with recent expenses, Mary and I decided to rent the empty room in our city apartment to Terence Bendixon, an attractive young Englishman and friend of the Winters, who was studying architecture at Berkeley.

❖

Despite our weekends at the cottage, I found I could do with exercise during the week. One evening after dinner, thinking of the courts near the medical centre, I asked Adrian, "Do you play tennis? Maybe we could get a group together."

"Great idea. I'll ask my friend Dave, and Mary might be interested as well."

Soon, we were meeting as often as possible at the hospital tennis courts after work, sometimes ending our day at the Russian Tearoom for borscht and blinis, as recommended by my boss Dick Grenfell.

With all this healthy exercise, Mary was becoming more relaxed. Her peach-like skin assumed its former glow. During our college years, Mary and Joe Sheen, her boyfriend at the time, had made a handsome couple.

After graduation, he headed for work in London, asking Mary to go along. She declined. I never thought much of it at the time, but looking back, I realise that Mary living with Granny Burke and her bachelor uncle was not the place to get support for such a romantic idea. I wondered if she had found a replacement for her lost love of college days. For some reason, I was hesitant to ask her.

❧•❧

One afternoon, an unexpected phone call interrupted my thoughts.

"Hello," greeted the cheery voice on the other end of the line. "This is Fred Jameson. Berney and I are organising a visit across the Bay Bridge and on to the Napa Valley next weekend. Would you and Mary like to join us? We've found a place to stay. The conditions could be primitive, but I guarantee sunshine and good wine."

Saturday turned out to be dreary and wet, with a poor weather forecast. Mary had a prior engagement with a new friend, but I was ready for a break so I accepted, in spite of the weather.

Berney Marchant was a large, solid man with piercing brown eyes behind thick horned-rim glasses. We'd met at one of the local restaurants and gone out a few times. He came from a wealthy family and went to a fancy Eastern college. At first, I was vaguely attracted to him, but Berney was spoiled rotten. He used to talk about settling down, but he drank too much and had no definite sense of direction.

Fred was behind the wheel when they came to pick me up that morning.

He supplied a reason with a smile. "Berney likes to talk and forgets where we are going."

"What's all this with the big car?" I asked him.

"We need to pick up other friends along the way."

Berney was in his element, entertaining us with stories of satirist H.L. Mencken and James Thurber, two of his favourite writers. Fred hovered over him, like a guardian angel. I was quietly puzzled.

In those days, even in liberal San Francisco, discussing homosexuality was guarded. Mary and I had been convinced that Fred might be gay, although not openly. My friend Dr Clare confirmed our suspicions some weeks later when we all visited her Lake Tahoe vacation home on Emerald Bay.

❧•❧

That morning, we picked up a pleasant couple in Berkeley, both architects from Switzerland. They were interested in my job at the medical centre. We also discussed Bauhaus architecture in the Bay Area and opportunities for jobs in California.

Our Napa Valley guest house turned out to be far from primitive. Used to sleeping on the floor since my arrival in the city, I enjoyed the comfortable bed and had no problems sharing the bathroom. We visited the Christian Brothers and Sonoma Vineyards to taste their wine – it was harsh and rough by today's more sophisticated standards. We picnicked on blankets and basked in the welcome sunshine. Even Berney consented to eating on the grass and ended up drinking too much wine. Since we were all feeling relaxed and sleepy from the fresh air, the trip back on Sunday night was silent and tranquil.

❖

The following week, I received an early morning call from my friend Adrian.

"I've just had a call from my old firm in London offering me a job with excellent prospects."

My stomach dropped. We both knew this would happen. I needed more time in the United States; he could never settle there on a permanent basis.

He continued, "We need some time together. Let's spend next weekend in Berkeley, see some Bauhaus architecture, and spend the night at the local inn."

❖

After breakfast on Saturday morning, we left the Sonoma Street apartment, the foghorn still booming as we sped towards sunshine across the East Bay Bridge.

"Let's enjoy every minute of our time together," he said as we checked in at the local inn. "I've booked a tour of the Maybeck buildings, and you have the map of the area. Be prepared for a long hike."

Complete with water bottles and a batch of sandwiches, we checked out the works of Julia Morgan, the first female architect in California, who designed a vast number of buildings in the Bay Area, as well as structures by Richard Neutra, Walter Gropius, and others who fled Nazi Germany after the war.

161

My relationship with Adrian was a wonderful combination of friendship and combined interests. We both knew we were living in the moment but also that it would not end in sadness, just with a sense of sweetness that would be hard to describe.

❖

Time moved on at Telegraph Hill with the comings and goings of friends.

The weekend after my outing with Adrian, an anxious and tired Barbara Hippel came by for breakfast.

"My mother is coming to stay in a few days," she said. "I'm trying to wrap things up at the office because my boss was offered an overseas assignment. Perhaps you could help me out with her, maybe with an invitation to afternoon tea or a drive to your beach cottage. Mother is formal and old school."

I could tell from Barbara's voice that there was another story there.

The following Saturday, over an afternoon tea of cucumber sandwiches and eclairs, I entertained Barbara's mother, an older version of her daughter and just as friendly.

After the usual pleasantries, she said, "I'm concerned about Barbara. Enough unsuitable boyfriends! She needs a sense of direction. Two years is enough to sort herself out. My husband has insisted she return home and take an advanced degree in Philadelphia. I'm delighted she has a friend like you. I just hope you'll visit us in Bryn Mawr."

I felt sad when Barbara left, but something told me our paths would cross again in the future.

—❧•❧—

Yes, life on Sonoma Street was changing. The apartment block seemed overcrowded. Street noises and loud music were the perfect recipe for broken sleep.

Mary echoed my thoughts when she announced one morning, "I'm sick to death of sleeping on the floor, of having nowhere to put away my clothes, and of waiting in line for the bathroom. We need a place of our own with proper beds and a place to entertain our friends."

I could hear irritation in her voice.

We decided to move to a larger, more attractive apartment in a two-family house at 14 Taylor Street over the Broadway tunnel on Nob Hill. This place was partially furnished with high ceilings, large windows, and a separate kitchen. We hung our colourful Feininger print on the living room wall. Mary had the bedroom, while I enjoyed the firm mattress of a curious contraption called a Murphy bed. The foghorn still boomed as the fog rolled in, but sunlight woke us for early morning tea.

Our first guests were Fred and Berney, who helped us sort out furniture. A friend of Mary's presented us with a Siamese kitten. Nobody except Berney objected, and he got little sympathy!

"Just keep away from him," advised Fred, who was already in love with the gentle blue-eyed creature we named Zavier.

—❧•❧—

With no backyards, most city folk used their roofs for sun and relaxation. In addition to our personal space, the house had a small apartment occupied by Styles Dickinson, a delightful elderly English gentleman who was an expert in ceramic work.

"If you are away for the weekend or go on vacation, I am happy to take care of your kitten," he told us. "As you can see, I have two cats of my own."

❧❦❧

We faced other new challenges, like learning to park the car on steep hills or finding the best corner market. The streetcar I used to get to the hospital had a stop at the bottom of Lombard Street, one of San Francisco's steepest hills. A worthwhile walking challenge in itself, the trek was better exercise but not so much fun as tennis!

By now, Mary was seeing more of Dave, Adrian's friend from Sonoma Street days. They often left town together or stayed at his apartment. I asked no questions, but I knew she was happy and content. Dr Clare asked us to return to their vacation cottage on Lake Tahoe. We also spent Christmas holidays with them in Portland, Oregon.

"This city is colder and damper than Dublin," said Mary, as the rain dripped down from the endless trees. The house smelled of pine and Christmas. I finally got a chance to ask Clare about my O'Keefe family in Wexford and her friendship with my mother Eva.

"Your grandfather never really recovered from the loss of his youngest son, Willy, killed in the Great War. He grew cantankerous and irritable.

"Whenever I would go to tea with Eva after school, I had to be on my best behaviour," she said with a chuckle. "Eva told me later that he never gave sweet cake to anyone he disliked. My eldest brother, your Aunt Daisy's first love, was also lost in that war. Later, Daisy became her father's best friend and confidante. Those were sad times. I will tell you more on your next visit to the lake."

❖

When we returned to life on Taylor Street, Mary was happy and often indulged her love of cooking. We managed to find a dining table at a thrift store, taking it home strapped to the roof of the car. Zavier took to sleeping on my bed and making friends with Mr Dickinson's rooftop cats. My cousin Derry made an unexpected visit from Dublin with his wife Cinnia and their five year old daughter Ann Marie.

"I got a temporary job in San Francisco and decided to see how I like working in the U.S.," he told me.

Derry and Cinnia were very sociable and often came to dinner. They enjoyed our crazy stories of Berney and Fred as well as discussing the Civil Rights movement, problems from the Vietnam War, and the changing conditions back in Ireland.

Other visitors from overseas dropped in as the months slid by. I slowly mastered the climb up Lombard Street from the bottom of the hill to get to work.

❖

I returned home from work one day to find Mary sitting on the sofa, looking sad and miserable.

"What's all this about?" I asked her.

"I've just received a phone call from my old friend Hugh McDonough at Bord Failte offering me a well-paying job with a guaranteed pension. I don't want to go back, but something tells me I'd be unwise not to."

Bord Failte was the Irish Tourist Board.

"I don't want you to go either," I told her. "But remember that without a professional degree you have no security. Leaving Dave may be painful, but relationships, no matter how romantic, can be ephemeral, and time heals."

She nodded and proceeded to make one of the best decisions of her life.

I felt alone and adrift after Mary left, so I threw myself into a crazy social life. When work took me across the bay to the Berkeley campus, I observed protests against the Vietnam War and other government issues. In retrospect, this experience kindled my lifelong interest in politics.

Sometimes I would contact some Irish friends who'd settled with their families in the suburbs outside the city.

Vinnie O'Kelly, now married to a girl from the Basque country, was starting an engineering company with Bob Schoenlink. I was now part of their social group. Bob and his German wife Gretchen were upbeat and more grounded than my friends in San Francisco.

One beautiful Sunday afternoon I drove across the Golden Gate Bridge to Bolinas Beach to swim in the bracing water and stretch out on the golden sand. It's not the same when I go back now – something is missing.

After I wrapped up, I returned to the city. A note in the house told me to contact Mr Dickinson. The uneasy feeling that inspired made me run upstairs.

"I have sad news," he said. "Your beloved Zavier was forced off the roof by an angry neighbourhood cat and fell to the yard below. I knew you would want to say goodbye."

He handed me a small shoebox, where my darling puss lay at peace wrapped in a cozy blanket.

I thanked Mr Dickinson for all he had done, slowly walked downstairs, and burst into tears. I must have cried more for that little cat than I did when Mary returned to Ireland.

❖

After a few weeks of work, including a trip to Berkeley, I received a phone call from Chris Dardis, a classmate from UCD days, who now worked in Manhattan.

"Hi Eleanor, I've just received an excellent job offer from the Dublin Planning Board, something I always wanted," he began. "Are you interested in taking over my apartment at 12 East 92nd Street? It's rent-controlled at $100 a month."

"What a lovely surprise. I'd love to take over the apartment!" I responded.

"I'll leave the key with my neighbour, Dick Bauer, a pleasant and reliable chap. The next month's rent is paid. No rush on your part. Just mail your date of arrival."

The timing was perfect. I was badly in need of a change. I remembered how much I'd liked the apartment on my brief visit there while in New York with Roddy some years ago.

❧·❧

It seemed that the grant for my job was to expire soon. There was so much work still to be tied up that I was grateful for the extra time from Chris. Jack Wagstaff and Dick Grenfell gave me a great send-off at the Hospital, and my landlord agreed to let me stay until the end of the month.

I had a farewell dinner with John and Val Winter on Sonoma Street, telling them about my move to NYC. Things were changing with these old friends, too.

"We're also checking out," John said. "Things are improving in London, and I've had some job offers. But no sad goodbyes now. I have a feeling we'll all get together on the other side of the Pond."

My first host in San Francisco, Michael Graham, stopped by my apartment one day on his way back from work. He looked happier and more relaxed than usual.

"What's going on?" I asked him over tea and biscuits.

"Well," he said, "Pat and I are looking to the future. We don't want to grow old here, so we are planning a move to Europe. In essence, we're looking to build a small exclusive hotel at Porto Santo Stefano on the west coast of Italy near the port of Ostia, within easy reach of Rome. Would you consider designing the building?"

I told Michael about my impending move to New York. "I would love to, but there just isn't time."

He gave me a friendly hug. "I completely understand, but perhaps you could recommend another architect."

Michael, too, spoke of the future. "Perhaps one day you will come to visit! We are naming the hotel Il Pelicano after our house in Tiberon."

After Michael left, I called Pat Quin, a fellow countryman and Dean of the Berkeley School of Architecture. He was delighted to work with Michael and thanked me for the recommendation.

Fred and Berney treated me to a farewell dinner at a posh restaurant downtown, with promises to visit NYC.

Even Dr Clare approved of my plan.

"San Francisco is fun for a while," she said. "In Manhattan, you will find a real job and maybe a good man. Robin also sends his good wishes."

❧•❧

Looking back on those magical years, what I remember most is not the wild parties and craziness, but the start of lifelong friendships among three young women: Barbara, Mary, and me. Connections that lasted almost half a lifetime.

#12 EAST 92ND STREET

I climbed out of the taxi, weary yet excited. The air smelled of diesel and spring. It was mid-morning on a quiet residential block between Madison and Fifth Avenue. Apparently, little had changed there since my first visit three years ago. But I knew that I had.

Climbing up four flights of stairs there was nothing compared with the trek up the hill to my apartment in San Francisco. Besides, I was only carrying a modest suitcase. My two steamer trunks would arrive later. Dick Bauer, a tall angular young man with sandy hair, greeted me at the top of the stairs.

"Welcome to the Boarding House for Irish Architects. We must keep up the tradition," he said with a smile. "Since the 1950s, only Irish architects have rented this place. I'm a model maker and enjoy having them as neighbours.

"Don't hesitate to phone if you need anything." He handed me two sets of keys.

The apartment, a large, subdivided space with high ceilings and an almost floor-length window, was hot and stuffy. I opened the window. The scent of daffodils wafted up from the window boxes on the street below.

The scant furnishings included a few Eames chairs. Reproductions of contemporary artists' works broke up the white walls, and a faded Kilim rug covered the parquet floor. The bathroom sat just off the small kitchen and dining area, cleverly hidden behind a light screen set into the interior wall. My bed was a futon, and the other sofa had storage space below it.

Chris Dardis, whose apartment this was prior, had left some food essentials in the fridge for me. Sitting down later with a cup of tea, I saw he had also left a list of phone numbers – former friends who were now living in Manhattan.

The only familiar name was June Listen. I remembered her thin face with bright blue eyes set above a pointed nose. We had gone to the same parties in graduate school when she was doing her advanced degree in social work. I recalled that she had grown up in England and that her parents had retired to Dublin. But I found my eyes were beginning to close. *I must make up my bed. Tomorrow is another day.*

❖

Loud noises from the street prevented me from sleeping in the next day. A large garbage truck was starting to empty bins on both sides of the street. I closed the window, cursing the heating system as I headed for the bathroom.

The shower worked well, with the spray bringing me back to reality. What to wear was the next challenge. *No more scruffy cut-offs for me!*

My light tweed off-white coat seemed like a good idea to cover one of my few cotton dresses. It was still spring in NYC, where people wore suits or dresses for work.

I decided to phone June. It was still early, so I left her a message. My phone rang as I finished a cup of tea and a bowl of stale corn flakes.

"Hello, Eleanor. Great to hear from you. Chris told me at the last UCD party that you were taking over his apartment. I have today off, so why not come to dinner this evening? I'm only a few blocks away," she continued, "so it's an easy walk. This is a very safe neighbourhood."

I accepted the invitation, taking down her address and assuring her I had a map of the city.

❧•❧

On a practical level, I needed to find a few places – the nearest corner store, the local subway stop, and a coffee shop. By the time I was ready to leave, the garbage trucks were gone. I observed a uniformed doorman at the house directly opposite assisting an elegantly dressed grey-haired man with a heavy briefcase into a black limo. It reassured me. *These stairs may smell of stale cabbage, but it looks like I'm living in a posh neighbourhood.*

Thinking back to three years prior, I could recall walking from here to the Metropolitan Museum of Art on Fifth Avenue and the Frick Collection, even visiting Central Park Zoo. But those pleasures would have to wait.

I located a large corner store opposite the entrance to the subway on 3rd Avenue. Then I stopped to enjoy a coffee and English muffin at a Schrafft's nearby. Some women in the street were wearing white gloves – a tribute to Jackie Kennedy, who was known as a fashion trendsetter at the time.

❖

That evening, I had no trouble finding June's apartment on 86th Street after deciding to walk there via Fifth Avenue rather than Madison. Feeling energised and optimistic, I walked briskly as cars whizzed by and the lights from the tall buildings brightened the starless sky.

Dressed in casual slacks and a blue sweater and with the same mop of curly hair that I remembered, June seemed more self-assured and together than the skinny young student of her college days. We hugged after she took my coat.

June's apartment on the 12th floor had a bird's-eye view of Central Park. It was a bigger space than my pad on 92nd Street. The building also had an elevator.

"Welcome to the city that never sleeps." she laughed. "I'm lucky to be living here – it's been three years now!"

She continued telling me about her life in New York as we walked down the hall.

"I know Dublin is looking up these days, but work in my field is hard to find there. I've lived here for almost three years and was lucky to find a job at Sloan Kettering Cancer Institute. The hours are flexible and the compensation is good.

"Let's have a glass of wine and some cheese before dinner." She headed into the kitchen.

While she was out of the room, I noticed a familiar face in an Irish newspaper on one of the coffee tables – it had to be Ashling Harris, known for the large parties she used to give in her flat on Ely Place. She came from a well-to-do conservative family in Limerick. I had known her during my final year in architecture, a time of working long hours in the studio with no time to socialise. When June returned with a bottle of vintage Burgundy and assorted cheeses, I asked how she knew Ashling Harris.

"We were social work students together," she said, looking somewhat embarrassed, as if she didn't want to elaborate about their friendship.

I lightened things up and let the matter drop by telling June about my crazy time in California. It had been lots of fun – meeting some wild and wonderful people – but wasn't the place for me to settle down. I knew I needed to have a more balanced lifestyle with better job prospects. Until Chris called and offered me his apartment, I had even been thinking of returning to London.

Over a delicious dinner of Boeuf Bourguignon, mashed potatoes, and endive salad, we talked of mutual friends there and in Dublin. I learnt June had an older sister who lived somewhere in the Carolinas, and she also told me about her close connection to the Quinlan family in Dublin. We agreed to go to the next UCD party and maybe see a movie together.

❧•❧

Walking home along Fifth Avenue, I mused about June's connection to Ashling Harris, but then quickly dismissed it.

Woodsy smells of earth and loam wafted from the park. *Am I already starting to feel more a part of this restless city? Maybe it's just the joy of meeting an old friend.*

❖

Finding work in New York was less of a challenge than it had been on the West Coast. The head-hunter recommended by Chris, a comfortable woman in a tight black dress and wearing several strands of pearls, was organised and helpful.

I told her about my work with the University of California Medical Centre.

"Building is booming, your credentials are great, and there's plenty of work, but I'd like to find you a comfortable environment. Women are still rare in the field," she said. "Rogers & Butler – they specialise in hospital work, perfect for you – has a big contract coming up in August. I know they would like you, but, for now, I'll find a temp job to tide you over. Living in New York City is expensive."

❖

The temp job in a medium-sized architects' office between 3rd and Lexington turned out to be casual and friendly. Everyone there was Jewish except Lennie, a funny British chap from South London.

Lennie and I would tell each other jokes that nobody but us understood; they all laughed anyway. The two partners of the firm argued about everything, but never held grudges. The work itself was rather dull, mainly plants for refrigeration on Long Island, but I wasn't one to complain. It was nice to be back working on the drawing board.

I usually took the subway to work but walked home, wending my way through one street and then another, past the monumental Public Library and the large department stores on 5th Avenue. I loved the street noises, the smells from sidewalk vendors, the ambulances and fire trucks screeching through the traffic. The energy of that vibrant city released tensions I didn't know I'd held onto. Unexpected views of the East River flashed through the side streets. After 56th Street, lower buildings with small shops replaced large commercial structures.

Nearer to home, I turned west onto the quiet residential streets. Street cleaners were out, gardeners were watering flower boxes, and the air smelled of Clorox and Spring. Well-dressed mothers pushed elaborate strollers. Uniformed schoolchildren from private schools in the neighbourhood giggled and laughed together on their way home.

I picked up eggs and cheese at the corner store. Across the street, an Indian woman strumming a zither stopped her playing to sell me flowers. I bought a bunch of yellow tulips; she smiled and thanked me.

◆⋅◆

This particular day brought no interesting mail, except a note from Yvonne Westfried, who had sponsored my trip to the U.S.

I hadn't seen her since I'd visited New York three years before and been to her house for dinner. I hadn't wanted to phone her until I had a secure job, so I found myself wondering how she knew I was back in town.

Sitting down at home after a glass of wine and a modest supper of scrambled eggs and crusty bread, I felt more relaxed and decided to phone Yvonne. I remembered that the Westfrieds dined early, so they ought to have been finished, as it was almost 8pm.

Yvonne sounded chipper as ever, explaining that she had received a letter from a friend of my cousin Roddy telling her my date of arrival.

"Ernest is not well," she replied, after I asked about her husband. "He fell off his horse in Central Park and injured his back, but thankfully had no broken bones."

She didn't sound too bothered by this and swiftly changed the subject. "I would love to take you to dinner and hear about your time in California. I'm sure much has changed since my visit there ten years ago."

We agreed to see each other at the end of the week.

❧❦

The end of the week came around quickly, and she picked me up in a taxi around 6:30pm. When she stepped out to meet me, she was the same diminutive figure with sparkling blue eyes that I remembered, wrapped in a black squirrel jacket. I felt dowdy and unfashionable in my light tweed coat.

We greeted each other in the French style, with a kiss on each cheek before stepping into the cab. The scent of Chanel filled the air around us.

"Please drop us at the Veau D'Or on East 60th Street," Yvonne said to the driver.

Turning to me she said, "If you like French food, this is the best place to dine."

It was still bright when we arrived at our destination. The Veau D'Or was a small unpretentious place tucked into a narrow street of equally small restaurants, its gilded sign the only indication of its class. I was excited and hungry. The white tablecloths and appointments reminded me of a childhood trip my family had taken to Royon, a seaside resort on the French southwest coast, before the war. I remembered my father, a serious Francophile, lamenting that we only had one French restaurant in the whole of Dublin.

The maître d' ushered us to the table. It was clear, watching them chatter with each other, that Yvonne was a habitué here. She headed straight to her favourite place against one of the side walls. The waiter recommended a *Potage au Cresson*, cream of watercress soup, followed by *Thon á la Provençale* as the main course.

"I'm a light eater and tend to order fish, but maybe you would prefer something else?" Yvonne remarked to me.

"Absolutely not, your selection is perfect."

Over a glass of chilled Mâcon, we chatted about San Francisco. I shared my observations.

"It was a magical place, so different from a Europe still recovering from the war," I said. "I met some wonderful young people, mostly trying to find themselves, but nobody I would like to spend the rest of my life with. It's a sort of Peter Pan land. Opportunities are limited, and women in architecture are still unrecognised."

The topic changed to family. I asked her about her children, her daughter and her son Tommy, whom I met briefly on my first visit to Manhattan.

"At the end of the war, Paris was occupied by the Germans, and so we had to leave. Ernest, as you know, is Jewish," she began.

"My beautiful daughter Arlette, who worked for the French government, was living with her Russian lover in Montmartre. He was suspected of being a spy. The situation was chaotic; everything happened so quickly. Arlette was reluctant to leave, assuring us she would follow when things got better. But she never arrived. We made all sorts of inquiries over the years, but to no avail. These were difficult times in Europe. She was probably incarcerated along with her Russian boyfriend."

I could see the tears in her eyes and took her hand.

"It all seems like a bad dream," she said. "But there's no looking back. Life has been good in other ways. Ernest and I have had a good life together. He did have affairs, but he always returned to me. When the chips were down, the family came first. I learned to accept his ways. The French have a better way of dealing with infidelities. Americans run to the divorce court."

Changing tone, she said, "Let's order dessert, and I will tell you something about your father's family that you should know about.

"I was at École du Sacre Coeur in Montmartre with your aunt Clare McArevey. Because of my connection with the Donnellys, her mother's family, Clare and I became friends. She was the eldest child of the family; your papa Bertie was the youngest. I felt sorry for this frail and lonely girl, in poor health and needing medical attention. There was talk of her father coming to visit her, but he never arrived. She developed tuberculosis and died shortly after afterwards."

I told her that I knew one of my Daddy's sisters died in Paris, but he always refused to discuss it.

"Thank you for telling me what you remember of the story. I'm sure there was plenty of guilt in the family. On my next visit to Ireland, I will try to research what really happened," I said.

FIRE ISLAND, A WEEKEND OASIS

The walk home from work was always exhausting. As soon as I got home, I would throw my jacket on the bed, open a window, and grab a glass of water. *It's still only June – how will I ever survive the summer in this stuffy apartment?*

One afternoon, I was shaken from these thoughts by the ringing of the phone. I didn't feel like talking but answered anyway.

"It's Dick from next door," a man's voice began, "I'm having a few friends over this evening for wine and snacks, any time after eight, informal. I'd love you to join us."

I said yes without much thought. His apartment faced north and ought to be cooler than mine. There was a possibility he might even have an air conditioner. So, an hour later, I knocked on the door of Dick's apartment, hearing English voices and the clink of glasses from inside. *Yes, his space seems much cooler and larger than mine.*

It was a very masculine room, with off-white walls and little furniture except for the large rectangular work-table he'd cleared off for the party.

"Eleanor, meet my English friends, Penny and Heather. This is Eleanor, my new neighbour. She's an architect, just arrived from California by way of London and Dublin."

Penny was a petite blonde with an English-rose complexion. She was also a newcomer to New York and had just got a job with Elizabeth Arden. Heather was elegant and tall with long black hair and violet eyes. She worked in graphic design. Most of the group was casually dressed and seemed to know each other. I turned to see a young man with a shy smile wearing a pink shirt who urged me to try the dish bubbling at the end of the table.

"This fondue is very tasty and all the rage now," he said. "I'm Ed Stennis, an old friend of Dick's. I work for the Federal Government."

Just then, Dick called for our attention.

"It's still June," Dick began. "But as you all know, it can be unpleasant here in July and August. This year, we're renting the same cottage on Fire Island. If any of you are interested, my friend Ed, here, will give you all the details ..."

Penny and I were curious. Where was this island and how could we get there? Feeling relaxed and cool after our glasses of chilled Prosecco and some of the yummy fondue, we decided to find answers.

According to Ed, Fire Island was one of several small barrier islands off the south coast of Long Island. Without cars, shops, or commercial business, it was a mecca for city dwellers during the summer months and was easily reached by ferry from Patchogue, a stop on the Long Island Railroad.

"Dick and I started going there a few years ago and decided to invite our city friends to join us. It's a very loose, informal arrangement so that young working singles can meet one another on weekends," Ed told us.

"You can come alone or with a friend. Dick takes care of the house details, and I'm the finance guy. Members pay $100 for the season and $25 extra when you bring a visitor. It's advisable to book ahead."

Penny and I signed up with him right away for the first weekend in July before we rejoined the rest of the party. Now I had a solution for my stuffy apartment!

❧⋅❧

The next day brought a long letter from my old friend, Mary King, now back in Dublin.

> *The job with the Irish Tourist Board is terrific! I've just put a down payment on a small house in Sandymount and have been appointed to check out the Irish Embassies in Europe.*
>
> *Life is good.*
>
> *Thank you for advising me to return home.*

I was suddenly struck by nostalgia for our crazy time in San Francisco. But I was running late for work and couldn't afford to dwell.

❧⋅❧

My office was air conditioned; however, it did nothing to alleviate my struggle with the dreary drafting job.

That morning, Lennie, my British buddy, was discussing news about the Civil Rights movement and the partners a plan for their summer vacation in the Catskills, when suddenly my phone interrupted us.

"It's Meg, your friendly head-hunter," said the cheery voice on the other end of the line. "Remember that big job I told you about—at Rogers & Butler? Well, it may start pretty soon. Are you free for an interview this week?"

We agreed to a time, and she gave me the address: 330 East 34th Street.

❧·❧

When the time came around, I was excited about the interview and decided to wear a tailored cotton dress and proper shoes. The office, close to Fifth Avenue, was in a medium-height classical building, unpretentious but still making a statement.

A pretty receptionist with curly blonde hair assigned me a seat in the large entrance hall, announcing in a foreign accent, "Mr Rogers will be with you in a few minutes."

When James Gamble Rogers came out to meet me, he extended a strong hand for me to shake. He was a handsome man in a tweed jacket and yellow tie. He seemed relaxed and eager to talk about his architectural achievements.

The first Mr Rogers was born in 1867, and since he started the firm, it had remained in the family, designing hospitals, schools, and important public buildings. The first Mr Rogers could have been the present Mr Roger's father, but I wasn't certain, and I never asked.

The office was comfortable and cool with sturdy furniture. Framed architectural drawings of large modern buildings broke up the green office walls.

"Tell me about your job at UC Medical Centre. I'm always interested to hear what's happening on the West Coast," he said.

"My job was mostly about communication between the hospital and outside architects. It was a friendly place to work, but now I am eager to get back to the drawing board," I told him.

"We are starting work on a new wing at the Presbyterian Medical Centre and need lots of help with the design and structural drawings. Eleanor, I look forward to having you as a part of our team. We work from nine to six, with double pay for overtime. You will have many site visits. How soon could you start?"

I assured him I could begin the next week.

❧•❧

Leaving the office, I was elated at this stroke of fortune. The summer heat was building up on the street, so I picked up a fan at an appliance store on the way home. I was looking forward to that weekend.

A phone message from Penny assured me that we were all set for Fire Island.

I had another message from June Listen, telling me she was going out of town for a few weeks. She didn't say anything else, which set off my curiosity. *Could it have something to do with the elusive Ashling Harris?*

❧•❧

That Saturday, I stuffed a few clothes into a backpack. Dressed in jeans and a long-sleeve T-shirt, I left for Grand Central Station to meet Penny. Our train was so crowded that conversation was impossible, but the Patchogue stop wasn't far away. We bought food at a large supermarket close to the railroad and wheeled our shopping cart over tracks and across the gangplank to our ferry.

A large truck collected our shopping. A gentle breeze rocked the small boat. The air smelled of diesel and kelp. At the dock, we gathered our shopping bags off the truck and started walking along the wide road that circled Fire Island. Each cottage had a signposted number. Ours was #26, so we had quite a way to walk.

"I'm totally exhausted! There's got to be an easier way to get here!" said Penny, as she finally dropped her shopping bag onto the stoop of our sprawling shingled bungalow, which was surrounded by sage bushes and stunted pines. Ed, wearing shorts and a Yankee baseball cap, greeted us at the door.

"You gals look totally whacked! I should have told you to stay on that island truck. It drops off ferry passengers and their luggage for free."

I felt cranky and worn out but eager to get on with the day. Ed went on to tell us that there was a full house that weekend, but since we'd arrived early, we'd get our choice of bedroom.

"Take your time and unwind," he continued. "We don't eat until everyone arrives."

As we unpacked our stuff, I got to know Penny a bit better and asked why she came to New York.

"I come from a working-class family in Birmingham. My dad was a cop, and my mother stayed home. I was lucky to find a job at the local branch of Elizabeth Arden," she said. "They liked how I worked with customers, so they sent me to the main branch in London. I may return there, but not before I've seen more of the United States, especially New York City."

I took this time to ask her advice about skincare. She told me I had good skin but should always remember to wear a hat in the sun.

She then surprised me by saying, "And now I am going to pluck those bushy eyebrows of yours!"

❖❖❖

Refreshed and relaxed, we eventually returned to the living space. Ed, who seemed to be in charge of the kitchen, handed us each a cold beer.

"It's too late for the beach," he said. "I'm going to start the grill in a few minutes."

We helped Ed by making salads and setting the table outside the cottage. Dick joined us, coming out of the cottage with his guest, a petite young woman wearing colourful silk trousers and a matching tunic. She introduces herself as Maya Khoury.

"I'm here from Lebanon to study at the Art Institute," she said, smiling.

We were soon joined by Heather and her boyfriend Harry. Dick let us know another couple would be arriving on the early morning ferry.

As we were heading off to bed, he had a few last reminders for us all. "Breakfast here is on your own. If any of you are early risers and want a swim, just follow the signs to the beach behind the cottage. It's not full tide until midday. There's no lifeguard, but it's very safe. Don't forget tomorrow's story time after supper!"

❖

The next morning, Penny and I stuffed our backpacks, grabbed some breakfast, filled a small freezer bag and headed for the beach, an endless stretch of sand sweeping back to an irregular shoreline of decayed tree roots, shells, and kelp. The incoming tide lapped gently at the shore.

The long, almost empty, beach soon filled up. Groups kept to themselves; some walked or swam, some played frisbee. Others read under beach umbrellas. So, the day passed.

❖

After a supper of delicious beef stew and red wine, we struggled down the narrow path back to the beach and sat on chairs or stretched out on blankets around a driftwood fire that Ed made from the bits and pieces we found on the shoreline.

"It's story time," said Dick, looking at Penny, Maya and me. "We would love to hear something about you and what brings you to New York City."

Each of us had different reasons for arriving in the big city. Maya came for further education and freedom from her conservative family, Penny, for adventure. I needed to further my career, and the offer of a rent-controlled East Side apartment was hard to refuse.

The conversation turned to books. Each of us shared a favourite. Ed was excited about *The Grass is Singing* by Doris Lessing, a novel about Southern Rhodesia. I joined him in his enthusiasm, confessing to having read it five years previously, when I worked in that colony after college.

Dick stoked the fire while some of the others went for an evening stroll. A crescent moon lit the darkening sky. The air smelled of sage and salt.

I shivered, gathered up my things, and headed up the narrow path.

❖

Sunday passed quickly with another relaxing day on the beach. After a late lunch, Penny and I took the early ferry to avoid rush hour, both mindful of starting new jobs the next day.

❖

Thanks to my new fan, I had a good night's sleep. Not sure about the dress code at my new job, I selected my best pants and a checked long-sleeve shirt with a black jacket.

When I arrived, the pretty receptionist greeted me once again with a friendly smile. This time, she introduced herself,

"My name is Irena Urban. Since Mr Rogers is running late this morning, let me find you a locker in the women's rest room."

She led me through to the rest room. It was a large space with warm red walls and bathrooms, set just off the entrance hall. A few comfortable chairs and a coffee table, as well as a small refrigerator, made it a pleasant retreat.

"I often have lunch here when we're busy and I'm too tired to go out," Irena said.

When we headed back to the office, Mr Rogers was waiting for me.

He introduced me to Keith Manning, a tall man with craggy features and a mop of curly black hair.

"I'm pleased to have a female architect in the office. I think you are the first during my time. We are a group of four. Luigi Salvatore works with the city planning department, and Jim Corbet is our contact with the engineering group," Keith said.

"You and I will do the design work. The firm likes us to dress more formally for site visits, but in the drafting room, it's casual. Smoking is discouraged though.

"I would love to hear about your work at the University of California Medical Centre – how about lunch together later?"

I learned that lunch was a serious business in New York City. Eating at your workspace was rare. Whether you had a sandwich on the steps of the New York Public Library, ran errands, or checked into a restaurant, the office would empty out during lunch hour.

Keith told me he lived in Kingston, across the Hudson River. His wife taught elementary school maths. They had two children, who were eight and ten. His whole family was liberal and into politics. We discussed my past work at UC Medical Centre, the place of women in architecture, and my luck at having a rent-controlled apartment on the upper East Side.

❖

The following week, Jim Corbet asked me to accompany him on a site visit to Presbyterian Hospital. We took the subway, reaching the construction site in record time. Jim left me to make my own observations. As for the construction workers, they answered my questions but seemed uneasy working with a woman.

I made my notes and had lunch in the hospital dining room, which reminded me of my time at the UC Medical Centre in San Francisco, but, here again, the atmosphere was more rushed and noisier.

❧❧

After a few weeks, most of the guys regarded me as a colleague rather than a curiosity. I had no shortage of invitations to lunch, though sometimes I'd beg off, eating an apple and granola bar on the steps of the New York Public Library instead. My workdays were long often it was after 11:00pm before I got home – but the firm always paid for a taxi.

Though it was still summer, there was little time for a social life during the week. I looked forward to my weekends on Fire Island, asking June Listen to join me as my guest one weekend.

While we were catching up, I asked her to fill me in on what was going on in her life.

"You don't look well, June," I began.

"Yes, I'm totally exhausted! I think you should know what my summer was all about. This spring, Ashling Harris called and asked me to find her a job in New York City." June seemed relieved to talk about it.

"I'm quite happy living alone, but I offered to have her stay with me on a temporary basis. Well, it turned out that she was pregnant and needed an excuse to leave Ireland."

June relayed their conversation. "'My parents are so conservative,' Ashling told me, 'that they would disown me and would never consent to my having an abortion. But I've made another plan. I know a couple in Chicago, and they have agreed to formally adopt the child.'

"When you came for dinner that first time, Eleanor, Ashling happened to be staying with some friends on Long Island. After that, I went with her to Chicago. Her health wasn't good, and the delivery was difficult, so, of course I had to stay a few extra days – as long as she needed me. The couple was lovely and delighted with the baby, whom they legally adopted."

"I thought something strange must be going on," I told her. "I'm pleased you've told me."

❧

Years later, when I was married with two small children in tow, I bumped into Ashling during a trip to London. She appeared as glamorous as ever, introducing me to her husband, a distinguished-looking Englishman.

I thought to myself, *There's an ironic twist to every story, isn't there?*

THE TRAGEDY THAT STOPPED A NATION

The change in season brought me renewed energy. A cool fall breeze would now waft in through the open window. I was still busy with work at Rogers & Butler, though with fewer late nights at work.

A letter from my old friend Barbara Hippel suggested I think about a weekend visit to Philadelphia. She had completed her Master of Education and wanted to teach elementary school French.

I would have loved to visit her in Philly, but it had to wait until I'd sorted out my life in New York.

June was eager to return to the social scene after her long stressful summer in Chicago. I accepted her invite to attend a UCD party the following Friday.

❧•❧

"Do these parties ever include Americans?" I asked her on our long subway ride uptown to get to the party.

"I doubt it ..." she replied. "Those I've been to were like old home week in Dublin."

Nuala and Peter Kenny, hosts of this party, lived on 3rd Avenue near Bellevue Hospital in a terrace of three-storey Victorian brownstones with high stoops and elaborate panelled doors. A buzz of conversation floated from their first-floor apartment as we walked through the slightly open door. Guests were gathered in groups around a large, uncluttered space with high ornate ceilings.

June introduced me to Nuala Kenny, a tall, elegant, dark-eyed woman with short, fashionably-cut black hair. The other members of the group seemed like a friendly bunch, mostly doctors, nurses, and others associated with the medical field – all very respectable. A few men wore suits, some tweed jackets, but they all had ties on.

Nuala seemed eager to fill us in.

"I'm a nurse working in the operating room at Bellevue Hospital. June tells me you are an architect, originally from Dublin. It's nice to meet someone from another profession. My husband Peter is also from Dublin and got his medical credentials at UCD. Right now, he's doing cancer research at Sloan Kettering Institute," she gushed. "As for me, I grew up in Sligo. My family, the Flannigans, are a progressive bunch. My mother was the first Lord Mayor of the town, and my brother Plunkett is a lawyer who does pro bono work for liberal causes. I have two sisters here in the US. Melissa is a nurse in South Carolina, and the youngest, Pauline, is a successful off-Broadway actress."

Turning, she pointed across the room. "As you can see, over here we have an open bar and assorted snacks. Just help yourselves."

This looked like a hard-drinking crowd to me, so I settled for a vodka and tonic. June and I circulated, eventually meeting the host, Peter Kenny, a tall, fair-haired man with a cherubic smile and intelligent deep-set eyes.

"Aha!" he cried, "a fellow Dubliner! Blackrock High School and UCD! Welcome to the group. I'd like you to meet Derek and Margaret Jeffers, from that small state called Northern Ireland."

I could see a twinkle in Peter's eye. For some unknown reason, I felt drawn to Peter – not in a sexual way, but with a feeling that he could be important in my future. And I was right – Peter and his wife Nuala helped to organise my wedding.

Margaret was small and slight with a hesitant smile and a strong Northern accent. Slightly taller than his wife with a mop of unruly hair, Derek appeared self-assured and friendly.

He spoke up confidently. "We've only been here for a month and have an apartment on the West Side. We also have a six year old son, Richard. Margaret's a pathologist at the Lenox Hill Hospital. I'm a technical writer still looking for work, preferably relating to medical technology."

"I'm curious how you met the Kennys," I said to Margaret.

"Queens University, Belfast, where I went, is affiliated with Trinity and University College Dublin, so I knew that Peter Kenny came here on a scholarship to Sloan Kettering," she answered. "We had no other personal contacts in New York City. He sounded interesting, so I just rang him up! Peter has a brilliant mind and a compassionate nature. We have a lot in common, and Derek enjoys his satirical humour."

The party conversation turned to politics and the recent Bay of Pigs disaster. Derek shared his strong views on the Kennedys.

"Jack really messed that one up! I'm all for Bobby, yet Jack is charismatic and good for the country, and beautiful Jackie brings elegance and culture to the White House."

Just then, I couldn't contain a yawn. Looking at my watch, I apologised. *It's almost midnight!*

"I would love to continue this conversation," I explained, "but I'm not much of a night owl."

I looked for a phone to call a cab, but without success. June suggested we take the subway.

❖

On the ride home, June asked me how I liked the party.

"I enjoyed meeting the Kennys, but as you predicted we might as well have been in Dublin. An American point of view would have broadened the conversation."

She nodded, and we agreed to give our social contacts some thought.

❖

Back home, my head swam with impressions and images of the people I'd just met. It was hard to envision small, hesitant Margaret Jeffers cutting up cadavers.

But, who's to say? I chided myself. My own profession of architecture was also not for the faint of heart.

⋙·⋘

The next day, my old friend Yvonne Westfried phoned inviting me to lunch on Sunday at her Park Avenue apartment. I accepted, hoping perhaps to learn more about my mysterious aunt, Clare McArevey.

Sunday rolled around quickly, the air smelled like autumn, and it was now cool enough to wear my off-white tweed coat over a silk dress.

Leaves floated and swirled like faded butterflies as I walked. Small children in their Sunday Best tripped along with their parents on their way to the park. I hadn't been to the Westfrieds' apartment since my last visit more than two years ago, but the uniformed doorman and fake flowers in the lobby looked much the same. A pretty maid with a foreign accent answered the door with a welcoming smile.

A blaze of sunlight brightened the large L-shaped room that was still filled with French and East Asian furniture. Heavily embossed plates and family portraits graced the walls, and a red-lacquered screen divided the living and dining spaces.

Wearing a fashionable light wool dress, Yvonne greeted me with a kiss on each cheek. Ernest, impeccably dressed in a tweed riding jacket and twill breeches, now silver-haired and somewhat stooped, kissed my hand.

"I'm off to the stables, Eleanor. I can't waste this wonderful day," he said by way of a greeting. "Yvonne would love me to stop riding, but it keeps me alive."

Shortly after Ernest left, Yvonne and I sat down to a light lunch of quiche Lorraine, green salad, and a carafe of Pinot Grigio.

"You look so much happier than when we talked a few weeks ago at the Veau D'Or," she observed.

I told her about my new job. "I'm in a large architectural firm specialising in hospital design. My colleagues are so congenial and respectful. With just a few women in my field, this is not always the case."

After lunch, I introduced the subject of my aunt to learn more of her story.

"My grandfather believed in a solid education for women, so he sent Clare, his eldest daughter, to Sacre Coeur in Montmartre, where you were also studying. You knew her through your connections with the McArevey family, didn't you?"

"Yes," said Yvonne, "we became close friends. She was lonely and delicate. Her father promised to take her home, but he never came. It was so sad. She died shortly after her seventeenth birthday."

Recently, I had discovered from continuing research, that my grandfather J.J. McArevey had brought Clare's body home to Newry and buried her in the family plot. Clare was born in 1883; my father, Bertie, in 1898. Clare died in 1910, when Daddy would have been twelve years old. *Why, then, did he never discuss this topic with our family?*

I had also learned from another of the McArevey grandchildren, who went to Mount Anville, a Sacred Heart boarding school in the Dublin hills, that the family had endowed a memorial window to Clare in the school chapel. I attended this same school in my youth, but never knew of the existence of this window. *Why was I never made aware of it?*

There may have been feelings of guilt, or other factors that perhaps I can never know. But speaking to Yvonne that Sunday, I was in search of more details about Clare.

"What were her interests? What was her fatal illness?"

Yvonne's gaze drifted to the window. "Clare was pretty and pale-skinned, with curly hair. She spoke perfect French and could be fun before she got sick. I think she had tuberculosis. She was always coughing." Yvonne drifted off then.

"Merci, Eleanor! Your questions about Clare bring back many memories of pre-war Paris, of my daughter Arlette, and the McArevey family, as I knew them."

The light was fading as I said my goodbyes. Preoccupied with thoughts of my lonely teenage aunt in Paris in those days before the war, I walked briskly back to my apartment. I shivered as I try to clear my head. Winter was coming.

Enough of the past. I thought to myself. *I need to get back to reality.*

❧•❧

When I arrived home, my calendar reminded me that tomorrow was Friday 22 November. I was conscious of the approaching bitter cold. *I must buy some warmer clothes.* With impossible deadlines and late hours at the office, I had little time to shop.

After a brief supper of canned soup and scrambled eggs, I tumbled into bed. *Tomorrow is another day.*

❧•❧

The weatherman had predicted a winter chill, so I layered up under my light California parka and headed for the subway. Irena Urban was there to greet me as I walked into the office, also stuffing her clothes into our commodious lockers.

"I've lived here so long," she said with a smile, "I forget how cold my Russian winters used to be."

And then it was back to the drawing board – there was a deadline ahead. The morning flashed by. We grabbed a late lunch at a sandwich place nearby and quickly returned to the office.

At about 2pm, news blaring from the radio brought everything to a standstill.

The announcer spoke gravely. "We've just heard from Dan Rather, our CBS correspondent in Texas, that President John F. Kennedy was fatally shot in a motorcade in Dealey Plaza, Dallas, at 12:30pm Central Time. More details to follow."

Mr Rogers entered the drafting room looking grimfaced and worn. "I think we should all go home."

We gathered our things in silence and quietly left the office. Tears streamed down my cheeks as I wrapped up with my scarf and gloves against the cold and headed for the bus stop.

The bus was full, but all the passengers seem quieter than usual, numb. A watery sun fought valiantly against the darkening sky. I needed to find out more about what had happened in Dallas. *Who else is involved?*

I needed to share my grief. It was still afternoon, so once home, I phoned June, who, despite the cold, suggested we walk in the park.

"I'm listening to the radio," she said. "I'll fill you in later. Come the quickest way you can."

I changed into my sneakers, grabbed a woollen cap, and headed for the bus. With no one in sight, I jogged along the sidewalk, which was almost deserted. June was waiting in her elevator lobby. Without much talk, we headed west to the park.

"What's happened since the first announcement?" I asked her, aware of the time difference. She told me what she'd heard on the radio. The assailant, Lee Harvey Oswald, a former Marine, was now at the Dallas Police Department.

"But that was almost two hours ago," she said. "The *New York Times* will have all the details tomorrow morning."

Exhausted after our walk, we finally collapsed on a stone bench set in a quiet corner close to the zoo. Our tears suddenly turned into ironic laughter.

"It's crazy, crying like this when we are not even citizens," I said to her, thinking of what JFK had accomplished for us in such a short time. He'd pulled us out of depression, prevented nuclear war with Russia, and so much more.

His famous inaugural speech was still ringing in my head. *Ask not what your country can do for you, but what you can do for your country.*

AN UNUSUAL PARTY, AND MEETING DON PRICE

After a dismal winter, the country was settling down. President Lyndon Baines Johnson signed the *Civil Rights Act*. And though the Vietnam War continued, it seemed very far away. The Beatles took America by storm.

Spring arrived with a flourish on 92nd Street. A warm breeze floated through the open window. Cleaning out flower boxes, gardeners chatted with the doorman of the house across the street. Replacing my winter coat with a wool jacket, I opened the window, scurried down the stairs, and walked to the subway.

Back in the architect studio, I found a note from Irena inviting me to lunch.

I've made reservations at a small Russian bistro on the Lower East Side. Let's meet there at 12:30.

I'd been curious about her background and was pleased she'd initiated the invitation.

The small Russian restaurant was almost empty. Smells of tarragon and dill wafted from the kitchen. Over blinis and borscht, Irena described her long, complex journey to the United States.

"I'm a Stalin baby and grew up in Nizhny Novgorod, a large important city on the Volga in western Russia. My father was a government official who disappeared when I was nine," she told me. "Mama, an activist schoolteacher, insisted I learn secretarial skills and become proficient in foreign languages. I was seventeen when we escaped to Germany by way of a peace program organised by the Quakers. With an unsettled government and the rise of the Nazi party, it was difficult to find work there." Her voice cracked with emotion.

She continued after a pause, "My secretarial ability helped, but we lived in constant fear. After almost two years of this, we came to the United States. Mother never fully explained how she initiated the trip, and I never asked."

"What happened when you arrived in New York?"

"Nothing was easy. We needed work permits and somewhere to live. Eventually, we found a rent-controlled apartment on the Lower East Side. I was a hospitality hostess on transatlantic passenger ships. Mama, with her language skills, was snapped up by the school system. After a few years, I needed a break from travel and found this job at Rogers & Butler."

I could sense the relief in her voice from unburdening herself; it was almost like she'd been to confession.

The conversation turned to me.

"How do I feel to be the only woman architect in the office? Hmm." I repeated her question and continued talking.

"Women are more accepted in Europe than here. I worked for two years in Southern Rhodesia and also in London after architectural school. Working conditions are better here than in California, though it has still taken a while for the men to accept me as a colleague. Site visits are still tricky though. The workers feel uncomfortable discussing construction problems with a woman, though I'm confident this will improve."

Irena glanced at her watch and quickly changed the conversation. "I love giving parties. It's so much fun mixing local friends with others I've met on my transatlantic trips. I'm having a get-together next weekend. And I figure you must be looking for a husband as much as I am."

I replied simply with a sly smile.

"I know it's short notice, but I'd love you to come," she finished.

I wrote down her address. Remembering Europeans liked to dress up, I decided to wear the new silk dress I'd just bought at Macy's. Since it was still chilly at night, my light tweed coat from San Francisco would be fine.

❧•❧

Irena and her mother lived in a medium-sized apartment complex built in the 1940s on the Lower East Side. The building had no architectural merit, but its interior, sparsely furnished with a few antiques and faded wall hangings, reflected an old-style elegance. As I arrived for the party, I could hear music, talk, and laughter. The event was well underway. A jolly, plump man with a curly black moustache greeted me at the door.

"Hi, my name is Echmel. I'm from Turkey. Come on in and meet the rest of the gang."

Irena, lovely in a green velvet dress, greeted me with a kiss before dragging me over to a young man standing in the crowd of guests.

"I'd like you to meet Henry Caldwell, a history professor at Columbia University."

Henry was formally dressed, like most of the guests, an international group of men and women, mostly professional in their late 20s and older. I met a visitor from China, two American lawyers, and Pauline Taylor, a tall angular young woman from Tasmania. Wine flowed freely as Irena's mama, in traditional Russian dress, offered the guests small honey cakes.

Henry, unable to shuck off the history professor in him, wanted to discuss the impact of James Joyce on Irish life. The lawyers ask me about politics in Ireland and why I had come to the US. The taller of the two had a pleasant voice and large, inquiring blue eyes; he captured my gaze. I asked him how he knew Irena.

"We met at a party on the *France* on my way home from a visit to London. My name is Don Price."

The other lawyer, Isaac Fishman, a bombastic and overweight man, worked for an insurance company. Pauline Taylor told me that she was a conservationist back in Australia. The party continued well past midnight. Isaac offered to take me home, while Pauline left with Don Price.

❧·❧

Next week at the office, I thanked Irena for the party.

"I saw you went home with one of the lawyers," she said. "I just wish it had been Don Price. He's such a nice guy."

I agreed privately but was hesitant to say so.

It surprised me when, a few days after the party, I received a phone call from Don asking me to join him for dinner the following Friday. I was excited and curious about the date.

❦

When the following Friday rolled around, Don was polite but more formal than at the party and didn't talk much in the cab. The restaurant he'd chosen, a small quiet place somewhere in the East Sixties, was elegant; the food was tasty. I could see he was a take-charge person who enjoyed good food.

He ordered a martini, and I settled for a glass of wine. The waiter nodded.

Over artichoke soup and shrimp scampi, I told him about growing up in Dublin during World War II.

"We may have been neutral, but with helicopters dropping Nazi spies into the German embassy and U-boats in the Irish Sea, we were deeply involved," I told him.

Don also talked about his life. "I come from a background of Welsh miners and German farmers – serious Catholics, hardworking and intelligent, but totally unlettered. I worked my way through college and law school at the University of Minnesota. Coming to New York ten years ago opened up a whole new world, the opera, ballet, and museums. Here, you work hard and play hard.

I have a challenging job at a white-shoe firm on Wall Street. The pressure of work is enormous. Sometimes you need to take a break, go to the beach, or for a hike in the country."

I noticed Don hadn't mentioned his family, and I decided not to ask. It was nice to hear him talk; unlike other lawyers I'd dated, he didn't boast about his own achievements.

"What do you think of Lyndon Johnson?" I asked him, taking a chance, since I knew very little about American politics.

"He's tough and ruthless in some ways, but he'll pass more legislation than any president in recent times," Don answered confidently. "He's messed up in the Vietnam War. But I'm hopeful. Minnesota is a liberal state where I've worked to elect Hubert Humphrey and Eugene McCarthy."

These names meant nothing to me, but his answer made me realise how important politics was to him. The restaurant was starting to empty out. It was cool outside as we hailed a cab and headed uptown. I thanked him for a wonderful evening. He dismissed the cab and gently kissed my cheek before offering to escort me to my apartment.

"Not to worry, I can walk home," I assured him. "It's just six blocks away."

❧❦❧

Don called again in the middle of the week.

"I know some wonderful places we can reach by bus outside the city. Would you like to join me next weekend?" he sounded keen. "Let's meet on Saturday at the information desk in Port Authority at 8:30am. I'll bring sandwiches."

Wearing a checked open-necked shirt and khakis, Don looked relaxed and comfortable when we met the next Saturday. We bought coffee at Chock-Full-of-Nuts and took a bus to a state park in the Hudson Valley. Except for my trips to Fire Island, I hadn't been out of the city since I'd arrived. As we strode uphill on a marked trail, Don told me he walked like a ploughman due to a birth injury.

"I'm not the sporty type, but I can walk for hours."

The air felt fresh and sweet, and it was lovely to see a baby rabbit hop across the path. After a long strenuous hike, we reached the top of the winding trail where the land levelled off revealing a splendid view of the Hudson River.

"Are you exhausted?"

"No," I lied, "but that was quite a walk."

On the walk back down the trail, we found a quiet spot to have lunch. He grinned and gave me a big hug. He was eager to talk.

"First, let's eat," he laughed. "There are so many things I want to tell you."

He spread a woollen blanket on the grass. We ate corned beef sandwiches and shared a light beer. Birds chattered in the underbrush.

"You should know something about my family. I never knew my father. My mother, Irene Seager, the youngest of a large farming family, ran away to join a traveling circus with a friend when she was a teenager, and that's where she met him. His name was Wilbur

Price, a handsome soldier who was AWOL from Fort Snelling. They fell in love and Irene got pregnant. Since she was only sixteen, her eldest sister Pearl Peterson took care of me. My parents stayed together long enough for my sister Lorraine to be born, then he fell in love with long distance. Family lore is vague on the details, but I ended up on the family farm in Minnesota, while Lorraine stayed with our mother in Minneapolis. I lived in a small town called Darwin with my grandmother in a one-room cottage until I was nine. Granny, who worked at the local woollen mill, was kind, loving, and a good cook. I went to the local school and felt different from the other kids, but never anxious or deprived."

Don looked at me and laughed. "How does my crazy story sound? Are you ready to take the next bus home?"

"No, I'm fascinated. My family has its own skeletons in the cupboard, but now I want to hear the rest. How did your mother make out?"

"She never finished school and eventually got a job sewing shirts for the WPA. She's actually still sewing for her living."

The sun was going down, and I shivered, looking for a jacket. *Enough for one day.* We packed up and headed down the trail. It was almost twilight when we arrived at 12 East 92nd. This time, I asked him to come in. He smiled, and we headed up to the fourth floor. My mind wandered back to my first love in Southern Rhodesia, when I was young and immature. Then, the stars were in the wrong place. But this was different. Now, the time was right.

❖❖❖

I began to see Don on a regular basis, depending on our work schedules. I couldn't believe I was falling in love with this crazy, complicated man.

He worked late hours during the week, though one night, when he'd come over early, I cooked him Dover sole in a cream sauce with asparagus. We'd splurge at the weekends and eat out in fancy restaurants.

He had season symphony and opera tickets. We discussed his frustrations at the office and talked about his friends, mostly lawyers. I shared more about my family, including that my youngest sister Esmay was coming to New York to visit and look for a summer job. He wanted to meet her and some of my other Irish friends.

❖

My sister arrived earlier than I expected. I found her to be much more sophisticated than I was at her age.

"You don't have to worry about me," she let me know. "I've contacted Doctor's Hospital. They've offered me a temporary job."

Doctor's Hospital was a private hospital for the wealthy on the Upper East Side.

"I'll only be here for about a month," Esmay said confidently. "After that, I hope to take a bus tour of the South with my friend Mary Ward, who's in Chicago visiting relatives."

The party I gave for her was a huge success. Thanks to Esmay's help, everyone mixed well: my neighbour Dick and his Lebanese girlfriend Connie, the Irish doctors, my girlfriend June, and Irena Urban. Don also appeared to enjoy our evening.

"I like your friends," he told me when we met later in the week, "especially the Kennys – Peter, with his cherubic smile, and the elegant Nuala. Perhaps we could go to one of her sister's off-Broadway plays."

Nuala happened to phone us the following day to ask us to supper, very informal, just the four of us.

"Peter so enjoyed talking to Don at your party, he'd like to get to know him better," she said. It was the beginning of a close friendship. We hiked with them on the weekends and went to the theatre and museums when time permitted.

❧·❧

After our usual emotional goodbyes, just before Esmay had left for her bus tour, she had given me a word of advice. "Be careful not to let that attractive lawyer slip away."

I'd laughed and agreed with her. A week later, Don proposed.

MARRIAGE, AND A LONG TRIP TO EUROPE

After the proposal, I began to think about the practicalities of getting married. How could we work it out? When my sisters, Ann and Mary Rose, had their weddings, I was living in Southern Rhodesia and not part of their large gatherings. Neither Don nor I had family members in New York.

However, we had no doubts about our relationship. *Why wait?* we thought. Besides, I'd never been into big weddings.

❦

Don came up with an idea which seemed to make sense.

He laid it out for me. "Instead of a formal wedding with all the bells and whistles, let's spend our money on a long trip to Europe, including a visit to Ireland, and later flying from New York to Minneapolis. I can arrange six weeks off from the office. You need to check things out with your firm."

However, Don did want to keep some things traditional. He laughed, "Despite my leftist leanings and crazy communist thoughts, I want more than a quick visit to City Hall."

"Fine. All this sounds easy, but without being regular churchgoers, where can we find a priest to marry us?"

Through a French-Canadian friend of the Westfrieds, I got an introduction to Friar Jean Lamont, a member of the clergy at the French church of St. John Baptiste on 6th Avenue. I had once attended Mass there and remembered its elegant classical interior and beautiful glass chandeliers. So, on a bitterly cold winter afternoon, we first met Jean Lamont, a short, youngish, brown-eyed man with a friendly face, who gestured at his thick green sweater worn over his clerical garb.

"I grew up in Marseilles and hate cold weather," he explained.

After we discussed our plan, he agreed to marry us.

"Just don't stand up on a soap box and shout Soviet propaganda," he said with a smile. "You will also need two friends to stand up for you, and they should be Catholic, or at least Christian."

❧❧❧

Nuala and Peter Kenny were delighted to help us out.

"Please don't tell any of our Irish friends," we asked.

So, except for June Listen and Irena Urban, none of our friends had any idea.

"Remember, you are sworn to secrecy," we told them both. "The last thing we need are celebrations at the local level."

Apart from pressure at work, we needed to look for a larger apartment, renew our passports, and get the necessary documents together for getting married. The days passed quickly. We found a charming one-bedroom apartment with a small walled garden in the semi-basement of a Victorian house on State Street in Brooklyn Heights. Once we'd found a few new pieces of essential furniture, we planned to move in before we set off.

One evening the following week, Don phoned me from the office.

"I found an article in the *New York Times* this morning," he said, before reading aloud from the story. "'Free tickets are available to see the Council of Cardinals in session for the first time since Vatican II', it says. Are you interested?"

"Yes. I did see some reference to it in the local church bulletin."

A while later, we received the tickets with a message that affordable accommodations were available to Catholic and non-Catholic foreigners at a hostel run by Dutch nuns. Knowing Don's fascination with the theatrical aspect of the church, I agreed, with the reservation that I may doze off before the session was over.

But there was another caveat. Booking in to attend this conference meant that our marriage date needed to be moved to Tuesday of Holy Week. This change needed to be arranged with our friendly priest.

Father Lamont agreed to marry us on Tuesday, but without a Mass. Between arranging things at our offices and tying all the pieces together, we were both exhausted. I made plans to stay at the Kennys' apartment the night before the ceremony, and Don with one of his friends, Henry Dickenson.

❧·❧

I woke up bright and early, dressed formally in a light pink tweed suit and trendy hat, had a small breakfast with Peter and Nuala, and headed to the church. Don arrived with his friend a few minutes later, looking uncomfortable in a dark suit, his pockets stuffed with papers.

After the brief ceremony and blessing, we returned to the Kennys' apartment for champagne and cake. June and Henry joined in the celebration.

Before heading to the airport, we changed into casual clothes, and I phoned my mother. Instead of scolding me, she was delighted and said she was looking forward to seeing us soon.

Arriving in Rome in the early dawn, we headed straight to a hotel in the Campitelli district, which is the location of the Forum and Colosseum, the Pantheon and other pre-historic sights. Though we'd both visited Rome before, there were always more places to explore. After our first strenuous day of sight-seeing, we returned to the hotel, tired and cranky. After a long nap and a dinner of red wine and pasta at a neighbourhood bistro, we were smiling again.

Don took my hand and laughed. "The trouble is that we both look at buildings from a different standpoint. At heart, I'm an engineer, and you are an architect. These are closely connected, but I'm slow and tedious while you quickly get the picture and move on."

"Yes, you do drive me crazy, so how do we sort things out? What if I look at some of the sights by myself and others with you?"

We both agreed on this plan, had another drink, and walked back to the hotel in the early Roman twilight.

I spent the next day looking for early Romanesque churches. Don, fascinated by the early Roman Emperors, particularly Marcus Aurelius, visited the sites on Monte Palatino. In the evening, we both agreed that our plan was working well and celebrated with a special meal in one of Don's favourite restaurants off the Piazza Navona.

❧•☙

The Vatican Council of Cardinals was a dramatic display of spiritual theatre. A panoply of white doves being sent into St. Peter's Square was beyond our expectations. Pope John XXIII, a jolly man, gave a brief homily of gratitude for the success of the meeting.

I could see Don taking in every detail. I, on the other hand, was appalled by this bunch of white-haired old men in charge of the church, thinking it was no wonder little ever changed.

My interest faded as the prayers droned on. All I could think about was food and my need of a bathroom.

❧•☙

We celebrated our last day in Rome at the Borghese Gardens, a place we both loved and had experienced on prior visits. Don suggested we have lunch and afterwards go to the Villa Borghese. More than anywhere else in the city, I felt we'd return here on a future visit.

Before leaving for Paris, we made a brief visit by train to Ostia Antica and further up the coast. There, my dear friends Michael and Pat Graham, from my San Francisco days, had built a bijou hotel some years ago for wealthy visitors.

As I'd predicted, they welcomed us with open arms to this elegant hotel with its broad-ranging cuisine, offering us the bridal suite.

❖❖

For me, Paris was a more familiar city than Rome, not just because I knew the language, but because I'd been there as a girl with my parents before the war. I'd also worked there as a student, spending part of several summers in a youth hostel on an island off Cannes with Irish school friends. Don, on the other hand, seemed more comfortable in Italy, but he had also been to Paris and was eager to see the sights.

We booked into a small hotel on the right bank of the Rue de Tivoli near the Les Halles district. For me, this was a new adventure compared to past visits; it felt a world away from staying in an old-fashioned hotel with my family or a scruffy hostel as a student.

Apart from a visit to the special stained windows in Sainte Chapelle, we agreed that Paris was all about visiting museums, art, and looking at modern architecture. As I expected, Don had booked ahead at some well-known restaurants.

Of the new contemporary sites, I was fascinated by the glass and steel pyramid piece in front of the Louvre, the work of Chinese American architect I.M. Pei. Don was more open-minded than I was and preferred the Pompidou Museum, which had been team-designed by Renzo Piano, Richard Rogers, and Peter Rice in 1960. On another day, we took a bus to Poissy to see Le Corbusier's Villa Savoye, built in 1931.

Now a UNESCO site, it's considered one of the best examples of Art Moderne of the 20th Century. Built of reinforced concrete, which weathers poorly in damp climates, it now appears run-down and neglected.

On our last weekend, we visited the apartment of a former associate from Don's New York law firm, who was working in the Paris office. Over an appetising lunch on the balcony of his apartment, Don asked him if he was enjoying working overseas.

"It's more open and relaxed than New York," Don's associate answered. "A long lunch hour is part of the culture. I think that work is accomplished just as well without the constant pressure we have in the United States."

❖

We said farewell to the magical city at a lunch party given by Don's Paris law office and boarded an afternoon flight to Dublin. We had aisle seats near the front of the plane. Don was immersed in an Irish guidebook, and I was battling headaches and nausea, grateful for the nearby bathroom. Don assisted me into my seat and shook his head.

"You should never drink vodka."

Knowing full well that I had a low tolerance for alcohol, I snapped back, "It wasn't the vodka, it was the horrible smoked sardines!"

Fortunately, it was a short flight.

<figure>❖</figure>

Aunty Daisy and Aunt Katy McCaffrey met us at the airport in a large taxi. I was not surprised that Mummy wasn't with them. Still nauseated, I managed to kiss their cheeks and let Don take over.

"Eleanor has a bad case of *la grippe*. I suggest we let her nap in the back seat."

My two aunts laughed and enjoyed chatting with Don on the long trip south across the city to Dalkey, the small village where most of my family lived.

Mummy, with her beautifully groomed white hair, greeted us on arrival. After we kissed briefly, I dashed upstairs to the bathroom.

"I don't think we'll see her for dinner." I could hear Don laughing while he sorted out the luggage and went to change into casual clothes.

<figure>❖</figure>

Later, Mummy and the aunts joined Don in a glass of sherry, followed by a roast beef dinner.

"We had a great time and some interesting conversation," he told me the next day.

I felt back to normal in the small semi-detached house on Hyde Road, close to Dalkey village where Mummy,

Aunty Daisy, and my youngest sister Esmay lived. Esmay had been out of town with a friend, which was why she hadn't met me at the airport.

Having lived with his grandmother as a child, Don was wonderful with older people. Mummy, whose idea of an American male was a gum-chewing, know-it-all guy wearing a cowboy hat, loved the attention from my shy and formal husband. He bought her flowers and chocolates, taking her for Dover sole in a high-end restaurant in the recently converted Dun Laoghaire station.

Before leaving for the West Coast of Ireland, Don and I took the bus into the city to visit Trinity College and the Book of Kells, the National Museum, and other sites of historic interest.

For the second half of our trip, we rented a car and set out for the long trek to the West. The narrow roads irritated Don, who wasn't used to driving on the left. I tried to keep my mouth shut and curb my urge to take over. Despite the ups and downs, we arrived in Connemara in the early afternoon.

As a wedding present, Mary Joan Trimble, a friend from architectural school, had given us a week at the vacation cottage she and her husband Gary had designed some years prior near the village of Roundstone. Known as the BOX, the small cottage was skilfully situated over a mountain stream that flowed into Dog's Bay to the south. Looking east, it afforded a magnificent view of the Twelve Bens mountain range.

Before looking for the cottage, we ducked into the only store in the village for some essential groceries. Sean

Maloney, a large heavy-set man with a twinkle in his heavily lined face, greeted us with a warm handshake.

"You must be the Americans taking over the BOX. The Trimbles told me to expect you. Mind you, I wouldn't have any part of living in that crazy contraption of a place, but I'm pleased to sell you some fresh local potatoes, carrots, and turnips," he laughed. "My niece, Mary O'Connell, cleaned the place up yesterday. She's the one to call if you need to know anything about the cottage."

Don asked him about restaurants in Clifden, the nearest big town.

"I can recommend a good pub there, but if you want gourmet, Cashel House Hotel is the place to go. It's a long drive, but well worth the trip." He handed us the house key and the necessary phone numbers. We were both excited and tired in equal amounts.

Apart from its clever design and amazing views, the BOX was amazingly comfortable with good insulation against the damp Irish climate. The next morning, we swam in the chilly waters of Dog's Bay with cows munching grass beside us. We explored Clifden with its music and pubs.

Before returning to Dublin, Don suggested we make the long drive south towards Galway to try out Cashel House Restaurant and maybe stay overnight. I informed Sean Maloney's niece of our plans, though for some reason, I felt uncomfortable about the trip.

Cashel House lived up to our expectations, both as a restaurant and a place to stay. Driving back, it was almost twilight by the time we reach the BOX, only to find its power off and the generator missing. The place was orderly with no sign of an intruder, so I phoned Mary O'Connell. There was no reply.

My next port of call was Sean Maloney, who was angry and upset.

"I'll get a hold of Mary! What is that *spalpeen* of a girl thinking of?"

It turns out that Mary had given the generator to some nuns while theirs was being fixed. A chastened Mary brought it back the next day. We really didn't mind not having a hot shower. Don saw the situation as part of our adventurous honeymoon.

"Now we have a good story to tell your mother and aunts back in Dublin."

Eleanor and Don, circa 1966.

VISITING THE TWISS FAMILY

The journey back to the Irish east coast was relaxed and enjoyable. By now, Don was feeling more comfortable driving on the left and had learned the tricks of managing the narrow roads.

"Tell me more about Ann and Dick. Twiss doesn't sound like an Irish name."

"Dick comes from an Anglo-Irish family. He was exempted from the war because of dyslexia and spent those years doing farm work in the north of England.

"After the war, he went to live with his mother at Rathleague House just outside the town of Portlaoise, which used to be very quiet. The House had many acres of rich farmland, which suited Dick well.

"Growing up, Ann was my nemesis. I was bossy, she was devious. Mummy was swept up with Mary Rose and left us to our own devices. Aunty Daisy and Daddy were busy at work and out of the house for most of the day."

I lost myself in recollections of our teen years. My sister had been the party girl. I was into study and college, while Ann had her own plans. She worked in The Country Shop on Stephen's Green, an establishment promoting Irish cottage industries, including a restaurant and bakery. I remembered its stark white walls and the pretty waitresses with red-linen aprons. It was popular with writers and poets, and I sometimes lunched there as a student. Ann also took a course in home economics; she did her own thing and did it well.

When she met Dick, I already had my degree and was working in London. I believed their introduction came from a friend at the Country Shop, though I wasn't sure. By the time they married, I was off working in Southern Rhodesia.

Moving to Rathleague House must have been a change for my sister. The house itself, a 19th Century mid-size four-square Irish manor house, was on an avenue lined with poplar trees. The public roadway to it was old and inconvenient. Despite its architectural pretensions, the interior could be cold and damp, but its kitchen, with an old-fashioned coal-fired range and flagstone floor, sounded cozy and warm. Help from the daughters of nearby farmers allowed my sister to enjoy the country lifestyle.

Though I'd had a brief vacation in Ireland about two years previously, this was the first time I'd seen Ann since getting married. I filled Don in on what to expect.

"Minnesota winters are intensely cold, but our houses were always well heated," Don said with a grin, as we approach Portlaoise.

The Twiss family gave us a warm welcome. Small and skinny in jeans and a green sweater, Ann was all smiles.

Her closely cropped red hair was already streaked with grey, and Dick, the epitome of a gentleman farmer in his Irish tweed hat and Wellington boots, took our suitcases. Two little girls were sitting on the porch steps. The eldest, Caroline, was a blue-eyed blonde with Dick's features, while her baby sister Sarah resembled her mother. We chatted for a while before Dick broke up the conversation.

"It's time for drinks and dinner. Enough of this chit-chat. Let's get the luggage inside and allow Eleanor and Don to freshen up."

Eventually, we reunited in the large comfortable sunlit living room, which had figured wallpaper and well-worn sofas and sat overlooking the front pasture. Portraits of stern-faced Twiss ancestors and hunting prints adorned the walls of the sombre house, which seemed more friendly and warm now than it was on my first visit.

I'd forgotten that Dick's mother, Emily, who was confined to a wheelchair, still lived at Rathleague House. She had a suite off the living room and rarely ate with the family except for dinner. Dick took care of all her needs.

He offered us gin and tonics, which I thought was a good summer drink, though I really preferred Scotch. Believe it or not, I'd switched over to Jameson since arriving back in Ireland!

Caroline told me about her new pony.

"Mum is teaching me to ride. And I'm not scared. Mum loves to hunt and has a big horse called Misty," she rattled off in the way children do.

I should have remembered that this was horse country and Ann was always a fearless rider.

Sarah was playing happily with a ragdoll on the carpeted floor in front of the window while Caroline chattered away.

Dick suggested we move to the dining room for our evening meal. My sister had gained a reputation as an excellent cook, and she lived up to it that night, serving a delicious Boeuf Bourguignon with garden vegetables followed by gooseberry fool with meringue and whipped cream.

Emily presided over one end of the table, Dick over the other. The little girls picked at their food. Sarah burst into tears when Caroline threw her dessert on the floor. Without raising her voice, Ann led them out of the room and returned quickly.

"Nelly will put them to bed," she said, referring to her kitchen help. "They are just over-tired."

Emily gave a sigh of relief once the children were out of the room, then turned to Don to ask about farming in rural America. Don explained that, in the mid-west, everything was bigger and more mechanised. While many farmers drove their tractors, the process was less personal. Changing weather and unexpected storms could ruin everything. Her face lit up with interest. I could see she was hungry for conversation.

❖

We woke early and had breakfast with Ann, Dick, and the girls at the kitchen table. Afterwards, we explored the stone-walled farmyard. Dick fed the free-range chickens, and Caroline collected eggs from the ledges and cracks in the uneven wall. The air smelled of compost and horse dung. Ann showed me the large flower garden on the south side of the farmyard.

"This is where I come to relax when the children are at school. Things get pretty hectic around here," she chuckled. "It took a few years to adjust to the country, but now I love this place, despite its many inconveniences."

Dick took Don on a tour of the other farm buildings and a walk through the kitchen garden. I was amused by how well they related to each other – two farm boys, one from the flat plains of North America, the other a gentleman farmer from horse country in rural Ireland.

We said our goodbyes the next morning and left for Dublin.

Ann and Dick in Portlaoise.

Eleanor (right) and Ann at the Twiss Farm.

ENGLAND: THE FINAL DESTINATION

Back at Hyde Road with Mummy and Aunty Daisy, we prepared for our flight to England the following morning. Don wanted to visit his old haunts from his post-war days in London. I was interested to see my favourite art museums and any major new construction. After that, we'd take the train to the village of Sevenoaks in Kent where my youngest sister Mary Rose and her family lived.

In Chelsea, we had a standing invitation to stay at my cousin Nuala's house, an 18th Century listed house on Cheyne Walk. Nuala was the eldest of my McArevey cousins. Her father, Jack, a successful Dublin barrister and my father's eldest brother, had died of pneumonia at thirty, leaving a young widow and three small children. His widow, Myra, went to London taking the little boy Eoin, but leaving the girls at a boarding school outside Dublin. My father became a father figure to these girls, who spent their holidays at Fitzwilliam Place.

Nuala never forgot Daddy's kindness and helped me in so many ways, both when I was a schoolgirl visiting

London during the war, and later, being responsible for my going to California.

I was surprised when it was Nuala's husband, James Allason, who answered the door. A Conservative MP, James was a tall handsome gentleman, formally dressed in a dark pinstriped suit.

"Nuala is at our summer place in the Isle of Wight, an emergency visit," he explained. It was something to do with leaking pipes.

"We are having alterations to the guest room, but the third-floor nursery is available if you don't mind slogging up the stairs. The maid is on holiday, so there's not much help."

Don and James took our bags up the creaking stairs of the old house. I was secretly pleased, remembering spending happy nights there after the war when the Allason children, Julian and Rupert, were little boys. I recalled a splendid view of the river and being amused by a red carpet in the bathroom.

James explained he was in London because of work.

"I would much prefer to be in the Isle of Wight, but duty calls. If you have a free afternoon before you leave for the country, I'd love to show you around Parliament. We could have afternoon tea on the terrace with strawberries and cream afterwards, an English tradition that might amuse you." He looked at Don, who seemed delighted.

The next two days passed quickly as we explored our old places, such as the reading room at the British Museum where Don had a reader's ticket. I remembered eating a sandwich lunch on its steps, before returning to my office job nearby. We took the Tube to Piccadilly, listened to a concert at St. Martin in the Fields and visited the National Gallery afterwards.

How much can you explore in one day?

I needed breaks for food and people-watching. My strongly focused midwestern husband would have walked forever, though he did remember we needed time for strawberries and cream on the terrace of the British Houses of Parliament.

❧•❧

Lieutenant Colonel James Allason OBE, a British Conservative politician, sportsman, inventor, and former military planner, worked with Mountbatten and Churchill and was the oldest living member of Parliament at the time of his death in 2011.

A TRIP TO THE COUNTRYSIDE,
AND MUCH MORE

After our visit with James Allason, we took a train from Charing Cross to Sevenoaks in Kent. I needed to get out of the city. Don confessed he, too, needed fresh air and was curious about the Hogans.

"Where did your sister meet Barry, and why are they living in a country village?"

I explained that Barry was an expert on wine who worked for a company representing Bristol Cream Sherry. Sevenoaks was a good alternative to London, much cheaper and with good schools. They had already moved twice since they married almost nine years ago and now had three children, Christopher, John and Alice.

❧

Mary Rose met Barry at a party given by the hostel where she lived when she first came to work in London. It was a real love match: Barry, an attractive young man with a public-school education, and my pretty sister,

237

both serious Catholics and politically conservative. They married in 1957, followed by a reception hosted by Nuala at her house in Cheyne Walk. At that point, I was on my way back from working in Rhodesia and was unable to attend.

Working in London, I met Barry for the first time at their flat in Croydon – a tall young man with brown eyes and perfect features, he was very upscale English and the perfect host. Chris was just a baby then, and Mary Rose, the perfect mother, looked happy and eager to show off her new-found cooking skills. Our conversation was mostly about children and family.

❖•❖

The Hogan house we visited in Sevenoaks was a typical unpretentious semi-detached structure with a small garden, not far from the railway station. Wearing a light grey turtle-neck sweater and matching trousers, Mary Rose gave us a warm welcome. Barry, still the perfect host in a tweed jacket and tie, introduced us to Chris, now a tall nine year old, with his father's good looks and twinkling brown eyes. Their younger son, John, a shy, flaxen-haired youngster, clung to his Mum. Alice, a pretty little girl with an English-rose complexion and her mother's large blue eyes, observed us with curiosity and caution. Chris took our bags upstairs to a small room under the roof looking down on a small kitchen garden.

Dinner was very much a family affair with sausages and tasty vegetables, accompanied by a bottle of red wine. The children, except for Chris, played with their food. Mary Rose gave them permission to leave the table.

"I can't wait until the holidays are over. Alice is going to school for the first time, and Chris will have football practice in the afternoon. John is shy and unhappy with his teacher."

I sensed her anxiety and made a suggestion. "Let's get a babysitter, and we'll take you out to dinner tomorrow evening."

She seemed pleased at that suggestion. Meanwhile, I was also excited about what the next day would hold.

"Don and I will spend the day sightseeing. I can't wait to explore the local historic sites."

✦•✦

We woke up early the next day, ready for our adventure. With the help of a National Trust guidebook, Don had already planned our day. First, we would explore Knole Park House, a former archbishop's palace built in 1455 in the Jacobean style and one of the largest historic houses in England. The ownership passed down to the Sackville-West family, who lived there until 1946, when it was handed over to the National Trust.

Don thought we might see the ghost of Ann Boleyn as we walked the many corridors of that ancient house. Although I enjoyed the tour, I was more concerned with Vita Sackville-West, who had been born at Knole and was the last member of her family to live there. A writer, poet, garden designer, and the wife of politician Harold Nicholson, Vita was very much a public figure and the first bisexual woman to acknowledge her affair with the writer Virginia Woolf.

In the afternoon, we visited the gardens of Sissing-hurst Castle, where Vita had lived during her marriage to Harold. The castle was not a significant building, except for the Jacobean bell tower, which was refurbished as their home. What we really wanted to see were the gardens.

Don confessed that all they grew on his family farm were vegetables and fruit trees – a flower garden was never included. Growing up in the city, Fitzwilliam Square had been my family's garden. Even though I do have fond memories of my grandmother's large garden in Wexford, I had never thought much about the plea-sure of creating one.

And there we both were, enjoying the gardens at Siss-inghurst with their themes based on the seasons (though a white garden had recently been added). The air smelled of roses and lavender. Small birds chattered in the bushes behind the pebbled driveway. Don was fascinated.

"Maybe one day we should make a garden. I love the tranquillity of nature, the smells and sounds."

❧✦❧

At dinner later with Barry and Mary Rose, Don couldn't wait to express his feelings. "I will never forget the beauty of those gardens, one of the highlights of our trip to England."

The following day, we packed to leave for Heathrow. Don admitted he was ready to return to New York City and a more regular schedule.

"We had a wonderful trip, but now it's time to go home."

I nodded in agreement.

BROOKLYN HEIGHTS, AND A VISIT TO THE MIDWEST

Although I knew we needed to visit Don's family in Minnesota, I really needed a break from travel. I also ought to have been looking for a job – though with lots of new construction going on, that could wait. Most of all, I wanted to explore my new neighbourhood, which was very different from #12 East 92nd Street.

Don and I were now living in a two-and-a-half-storey turn-of-the-century brick house, the west side of which faced the East River. The east side served as a dock for a private club. A foghorn lulled us to sleep when the mist rolled in, and the air was fresh and clean.

Our apartment at #6 State Street was small and could be entered from the street by a flight of small steps down to the lower level. The large living space included a wood-burning fireplace and a tiny open kitchen. On the west wall, a large French door led to a walled garden. Enchanted by our recent visit to Vita Sackville-West's Garden at Sevenoaks, Don was eager to create his own flower and vegetable garden and had already ordered large amounts of topsoil and natural mulches. Before returning to work the following morning, he suggested I explore the commercial neighbourhood along Atlantic Avenue.

"It's very Middle Eastern. I've eaten there several times. The people are friendly, and it's very safe."

❧

I decided to take his advice the next day and began my journey to Atlantic Avenue walking instead of taking a bus. Though it was still August, I was wearing jeans and a light sweater as I headed off past the law courts and other government buildings towards the commercial neighbourhood. By the time I reached Atlantic Avenue, I was tired and ready to eat. The combination of exotic smells, music, and laughter created a festive atmosphere. I felt safe as I sat outside in the afternoon sunshine. A smiling waiter brought me samples of dishes I had never tried before – tahini and baba ghanoush with plenty of pita bread.

"I leave my order in your hands," I said. "As you see, I'd like to try a bit of everything."

Sitting there, I enjoyed observing the smaller and larger groups in the restaurant and the variety of those passing on the busy street. By mid-afternoon, I was ready to take a bus home.

❧

Our life on State Street had its fair share of minor newlywed disasters. We asked our good friends Peter and Nuala Kenny to Thanksgiving dinner. I had never cooked a turkey before and, without much thought, sloshed slabs of butter on the breast with disastrous results. As the rooms filled with smoke, Peter, who had horrible allergies, retreated to the garden. Fortunately, he'd brought his inhaler. After a glass of wine, we enjoyed the rest of the meal, and everyone had a good laugh at my expense.

As fall took over and the weather chilled, I developed a nasty cough. Without a runny nose or fever, a local doctor ruled out the flu and suggested I was allergic to something in the apartment, possibly mould, since the place was below ground. After a second opinion from a specialist and numerous other tests, this problem was diagnosed as a definite allergy. The solution for me would be to spend less time inside the apartment. Going to work was the obvious answer.

Although I could have gone back to Rogers & Butler, I'd decided I needed a change.

***

Frederick Frost & Son, a firm specialising in schools for children with disabilities, was attractive because the atmosphere was less intense than my previous job. The firm already had one female architect and was looking for additional help. I was interviewed by Frederick Frost and his son Corwin, who were both flexible about work hours and time off.

"What would happen if I asked you for a two-week break to visit my new husband's family in Minnesota?" I ventured.

Frederick smiled and looked me straight in the eyes. "Don't worry. We're happy to take you on from your past experience in California and New York City. The job will be waiting for you when you come back."

❧•❧

I began working for the Frost firm shortly after that meeting, but it wasn't long before our travel plans were put in motion following a phone message from Don's younger sister Lorraine later in the same week.

"Hi Eleanor," she greeted me enthusiastically. "We'd love you to visit as soon as possible. All members of our extended family, including those at the farm, are around and eager to meet you."

❧•❧

After dinner the evening before we left for Minneapolis, Don handed me a glass of wine. We sat down, and he began speaking, choosing his words carefully.

"The Midwest is very different from our world here on the East Coast and yours in Europe. Minnesota is only partly a liberal state. Except for my mother and some of the younger members, my family are politically conservative."

"Don," I reassured him, "you must know by now that I thrive on new experiences. Besides, you've already put up with the idiosyncrasies of my family. It's not likely I'll flip about the oddities of yours.

"I'm glad for this conversation though. Since your earliest memories are of living with your grandmother, I'd love to know her family history."

"I thought you might be curious, but it's a long story," he said, settling in. "My grandmother, Mae Radell, married Frank Seger in September 1899. They began farming together in the small town of Bemidji and had six children: Pearl, Vernon, Art, Howard, Jessie, and my mother Irene. Then one day, Frank disappeared. Pearl's memories of her father are vague and disconnected. It wasn't clear whether her father just decided to skip out or drowned in the Mississippi."

He went on, "Grandmother Mae returned to her hometown of Litchfield with her children but got little help from her family. Her mother, my great-grandmother, Barbara Stiren, was living on the family farm with her daughter and namesake, Barbara, and son-in-law John Schulmeister. Barbara had always disapproved of Mae's marriage to Frank, even though she occasionally helped out with the children on weekends." Don took a small sip from his drink before continuing.

"There were other issues with this arrangement. Grandmother, a stickler for discipline, had problems with my mother Irene, who often stayed out all night. Then one day, at the age of fourteen, having completed the ninth grade, Irene ran off with a friend to join a carnival that was traveling through Litchfield. It was there that she met a tall, handsome soldier, Wilbur Price, who was, as it turned out, AWOL from his post at Fort Snelling. Two years later, Irene returned home pregnant, telling her family she was married, that she was leaving again and that she would return, bringing her husband home.

"Instead, Irene left for Minneapolis to find her eldest sister Pearl, who was living alone in an apartment and working for the telephone company. When Pearl and her fiancé Elmer Peterson discovered Wilbur was absent without leave, they recommended he turn himself in, which he did.

"Pearl and Elmer arranged for my mother and Wilbur to get a license and be married in the stockade with Pearl and Elmer as witnesses. Irene stayed with Pearl until I was born. With her husband in military prison, my penniless teenage mother was cut off from most of her family with barely enough money from her factory job to pay the rent for her small apartment, let alone the energy to care for a delicate infant," Don said.

"I was born in University Hospital on March 22, 1928. I was a sickly baby. How sick, I don't know. My first crib was a dresser drawer. Irene hired a babysitter for me during working hours. It turned out I was slightly crippled, with limited mobility in my right ankle, but that has never prevented me from taking long hiking trips, nor did it keep me out of the army, where I served stateside, teaching artillery, during the Korean War.

"When Wilbur was eventually released, he and Irene got together again and had another child, my sister Lorraine, three and a half years later. She was a happy little girl who had a good relationship with our parents. They lived together for a few years until Wilbur disappeared. My mother and other family members were always reluctant to discuss details about when or why this breakup happened.

"By this time, I had been sent back to Litchfield to live with my grandmother. Mae had little money and lived by taking in washing and, according to Pearl, making biscuits that she sold door to door. After living hand to mouth for some time, life eventually improved for Mae when she got a job as a loom operator in a local woollen mill and received her first social security benefit in 1935.

This money allowed Grandmother and me to live comfortably in a one-room house while my mother remained in Minneapolis with Lorraine."

Don had taken another break to have a drink. He continued, "When she secured a job doing piecework as part of a WPA program, Irene could also afford a better one-bedroom apartment in a converted house in central Minneapolis. She encouraged her mother and me to move close to her and rent an additional available room on the same floor. Irene was able to afford a full-time caregiver to take care of Lorraine. Later, Mother made a proposal to Grandmother that she would give up men and drinking. Using her pension and mother's wages, Grandmother was hopeful that this arrangement would make a comfortable home for the four of us.

"But nothing worked out as planned. The period when Grandmother and I lived together in that apartment, from Christmas until school got out, was the worst period of my life. Not only did Mother refuse to reform, but there was no community around us in the city. The house and neighbourhood were located in miserable slums. In contrast to the Litchfield farm and Mound, where Pearl and Elmer lived, the city schools were dominated by rough kids and bullies, for which nothing had ever prepared me.

"It would have been unbearable for me, if not for the Eliot Parks Settlement House's after-school activities. The place was quiet and orderly and had good counsellors and a lending library, which included classics as well as children's literature. Except for school, the Settlement House, and a quick trip to collect day-old Wonder Bread from the outlet, I stayed inside the apartment reading borrowed books and trash fiction accumulated by my mother. I did not complain to Grandmother until she herself found the situation unacceptable and wanted to move back to her area of Litchfield."

Don paused before continuing. "In contrast, Lorraine had a good relationship with Mother. They lived happily until Lorraine went to nursing school. She then met and married Jerome Koslowski, who came from a close-knit Polish family in St. Cloud, where Jerome opened his own supermarket a few years ago.

"After leaving the city, Grandmother and I returned to Litchfield, where I had been an excellent student. My aunts, Pearl and Jessie, and uncles, Vernon and Art, agreed to help me financially to continue my education. Then, when I was about ten, Mae died suddenly, and her brother, cantankerous Great-Uncle Tony, whom I disliked intensely, decided he would take the matter in hand and determine my fate. 'You have a choice,' he told me. 'Either you stay here and continue to work at the farm, or you go to live with Pearl and Elmer on Lake Minnetonka.'

"My choice was obvious, and one I never regretted."

By this point in his narrative, Don looked tired and fixed himself a gin and tonic.

"I hope this puts things into perspective. I once did a little research on Wilbur Price's background. My father was the black sheep of a coal mining family from Wales, according to one of his aunts. I managed to contact her and intend to do more someday. But now, I'm off to bed. Tomorrow will be a long day."

Flying through a clear sky on the way to Minnesota the next day, I observed hills give way to the flat landscape of farms and lakes. In about three and a half hours, we were descending into the Minneapolis-Saint Paul Airport. Don looked anxious.

"Let's look for Uncle Elmer. You may have to ride in a truck," he warned, as we walked to the baggage claim area.

I felt as if I knew Elmer and Pearl Peterson after hearing Don's stories about growing up.

Elmer was there waiting for us, but sadly for me, he was without his truck. Elmer was of Norwegian descent and appeared very much as Don described him: a moderately tall man with twinkling brown eyes and a big smile. This morning, he was dressed more like the chauffeur of wealthy women than a farmer. Ironically, as an odd-job man for the affluent who lived around Lake Minnetonka, that was sometimes his job.

After an hour's drive, we arrived at Pearl and Elmer's lakeside house where Pearl greeted us warmly. Don's aunt was a tall woman with elegantly styled white hair; she was wearing cotton pants and a colourful blouse with white sandals. The Petersons lived in an old farmhouse with a wonderful view of the lake. Elmer took our suitcases to the second-floor bedroom.

"We bought this place for a song almost twenty years ago. The renovation is ongoing. It has three porches, one with a glass front that reflects the winter sunshine. Don must remember it from previous visits."

We learnt that Don's mother Irene would be joining us for lunch. I began to hope this meeting might
improve Don's strained relationship with his mother.

❧·❧

For lunch, Pearl served a tasty main dish, which I would
call a casserole, together with a large green salad topped
with marshmallows and a hot potato salad, washed
down by weak coffee. No alcohol was offered.

Irene had arrived shortly after we did with a male
friend she introduced to us as Frank. Don's mother was
of medium height. She shared Don's large blue eyes, with
circles under them, and his light blond hair. But that was
as far as the similarity went. Her manner was outspoken
and direct, as if always looking for an argument. When
she questioned Don, I could see him wince and strive to
keep his composure.

As the meal drew to a close, Elmer offered to take us
for a ride around the lake on his pontoon boat, which to
me looked like a slow-moving dock. Everyone was ready
for a break by the time Irene and Frank left mid-afternoon.

❧·❧

The next morning, Don was up early. Elmer was already
out, and Pearl seemed more relaxed, drinking coffee and
reading the newspaper. Don wanted to show me the city
before we went to the farm, so off we went in a rented
car. The sky was overcast, but sunshine broke through
the clouds as we hit the highway.

"First, we need to visit Bridgeman's," he said, referring to the former drugstore and coffee shop where he

worked his way through college and eventually became the manager.

We received a warm welcome from the young woman who now ran the place.

"You are quite the legend around here, Don," she said. "Now, to show you our coffee is still first class, have a cup of our best brew and a fresh doughnut."

❖

As we continued our drive, I looked at the Mississippi River with awe and trepidation, imagining what could happen if it overflowed. Don explained its importance to the Twin Cities. Minneapolis was all business; St. Paul was the centre of government in the state.

Then we crossed the river and drove by the headquarters of the country's largest cereal company, General Mills, who produced products such as Cheerios, Total and Cocoa Puffs. The smells and images of toasting ingredients made me hungry. We found a pleasant open-air place close by and ordered a green salad and cold cuts with a glass of white wine.

Then, Don pointed out the Foshay Tower, the city's solitary skyscraper etched against the cloudless sky.

"I'm sure more tall buildings will follow. But now we have the Walker Art Centre, a reputable art gallery, and the Guthrie Theatre. St. Paul has beautiful parks and great architecture, but those can wait until our next visit."

❖

Don was delighted when his Aunt Jessie, the youngest of the Seger children and Don's favourite, called to offer to drive Don, Pearl and me to Darwin, near Litchfield, close to the family farm.

"I have a big car and love to drive. My husband Mac is at work today, and my daughter Kathy can take care of the house. Besides, I really want to meet Eleanor and have Donnie visit with our cousin Irene."

❖•❖

I felt a sense of peace in the emptiness of space as the vast horizon stretched on forever on the long drive to Darwin and the family farm. A sudden flash against the windshield and a distant rumble suggested a storm in the making. Jessie was careful, but it didn't affect the speed at which she drove at all.

"I don't mind thunderstorms," she told us. "It's the tornadoes that scare me."

Rain was starting to fall, and I felt a drop in the temperature, but by the time we reached Darwin, the sun was breaking through.

The one hundred and sixty acres of land that made up the family farm went back to 1878 and the Land Grant Program. The farm Don remembered was worked by members of his great-grandmother's family, John and Barbara. Their one daughter Irene inherited the farm when they died. Don had often helped out there but had decided early on that farming was not for him.

Times changed when the Schulmeisters' daughter Irene inherited the farm and married Vic Pearson, a much older farmer who lived in the vicinity. The pair went on to have five boys. Monte, the youngest, was now in charge of the farm. Vic lived in a nursing home, and Irene continued to stay in the old farmhouse. Don's mother and Jessie would stay with her over the weekend, and Don and I decided to check in at a local hotel.

Assisted by Jessie and other family members, Cousin Irene set up tables outside the homestead for a welcome picnic lunch of main dishes, local fruits, salad, and home-made apple cider. Don and I spent time there with his sister Lorraine, a blue-eyed woman with beautiful shoulder-length blonde hair and an easy smile. She had arrived before we had, to spend some time with Cousin Irene.

"The next time you come," Lorraine said, "you must visit St. Cloud and meet Jerome and my kids. I've given up my hospital job now that I have four kids."

I found Lorraine friendly, though very different from her brother.

Don spent the ride back to the city deep in conversation with Jessie while Pearl and I enjoyed a good nap in the back seat. Having visited other family members and taken more trips around Lake Minnetonka, I was starting to think about work and our life in Brooklyn Heights.

It felt like time to go back home. Uncle Elmer and Pearl drove us to the airport, all the while making promises to come and see us. All things considered, it was a happy time.

❧•❦

Back in Brooklyn, we found our apartment door swinging off its hinges, papers strewn all over the living room floor and the television gone.

The local police were not much help.

"We've had lots of similar robberies recently in this neighbourhood," the officer who came out to investigate said. "My best advice is to change the lock on your door or install an alarm. I will make it a point to check in on your apartment for the next few weeks."

Don headed off to buy a lock while I made an attempt to clean the mess in the living room until my efforts were suddenly curtailed. A sharp pain and nausea forced me to lie down, which was where Don found me on his return home.

He was frantic to make sure I was okay.

"Yes, I'm fine," I reassured him. "I felt the same way in Minneapolis last week."

I thought on things for a moment, before the realisation hit me. "I must be pregnant."

Don kissed my hand tenderly. "What a great excuse to look for a house!"

Lorraine and Jerome Kowslowski.

Irene Price.

PREGNANCY, AND LOOKING FOR A HOUSE

We installed a new lock on the apartment door, which helped me to feel safe, but the pregnancy was short lived. I miscarried the following Friday.

My doctor said it was quite common and nothing to worry about. Don was very supportive. To quell the sadness and get out of the house, I decided to return to work.

A phone call to the architectural firm of Frederick Frost & Son assured me that my job was still open.

❖

Walking across the Brooklyn Bridge on a cool but sunny morning the following week and navigating the crowds in the uptown subway, I once again felt the pull and excitement of the city. It was about a five-minute walk from the subway to the office. I took the elevator to the office on the third floor. Corwin Frost, the junior partner, gave me a hearty handshake and a big smile.

"Welcome back from your travels, you're just the person I need to see," he said. "Remember the School for the Deaf in New York State that you started working on before going on vacation? They're planning a new addition to the main building and hope you will continue working on it with them. Let's have lunch and discuss the plans."

❧•❧

The sound of Beatles music drifted out of the drafting room, which made me wonder if my young friend Gus Wormuth, a tall gangly fellow from New Orleans, was around.

I'd known Gus when I'd first come to New York and lived at #12 East 92nd Street. We'd met at a neighbourhood party. His soft southern drawl and zany sense of humour were unforgettable.

He came into my life again when I began working for the Frost firm and was my assistant on site visits before I went on vacation. He adored the Beatles. I was pleased to find Gus was still part of the office staff, and we were back working together.

Just that morning, he told me that he was now engaged to be married to a woman named Margaret, though he called her Peggy.

I was very happy to hear it. "Don and I would love to meet her. Let's work out a dinner date that's convenient."

❧•❧

After a few weeks in the office, my good spirits returned, and I was ready to face the outside world again. Some early morning sickness and stomach pain suggested another pregnancy, though, and a visit to the gynaecologist confirmed my suspicions. Don, always the naysayer, told me not to get too excited.

"Remember what happened the last time," he cautioned. "Just go to work as usual and get plenty of rest. Look after yourself."

❧•❧

An invitation in the next morning's mail distracted me from my personal problems. It was late fall and chilly. I needed to find a new outfit for a party we would be attending to meet some of Don's lawyer friends, so it was off to Loehmann's, the well-known discount store in Brooklyn, where I found an elegant light wool dress and jacket. A new hair cut on Atlantic Avenue also made me feel ready to meet Don's friends.

❧•❧

Since parking was impossible in the Heights, we put off buying a car until we found a house and instead just rented one for the weekends. That's what we'd done the weekend of the party.

Don's friends, Joan and Mark Frawley, lived in a large Colonial Revival house in a fashionable part of White Plains in Westchester County. The door was unlatched when we arrived, and I could hear laughter and the sound of clinking glasses as we walked through the door.

Joan Frawley, a small woman with smiling eyes and curly blonde hair, gave Don a big hug and kissed me on both cheeks.

"It's about time Don brought you to meet his friends," she said enthusiastically.

Her husband Mark, who was a nice-looking man though less exuberant than his wife, took our coats and told us where to find a drink. Don ordered a martini, and not being a heavy drinker, I settled for a glass of wine. Mark was happy to chat.

"I'm delighted Don married someone from Ireland," he said. "Both Joan and I have been to Dublin, and I have many Irish connections. Now, you *must* meet the rest the gang."

I sensed strong friendships among the guests, mostly lawyers, though there were two small boys, about five and seven, who were sitting on a sofa munching canapés.

Joan introduced me to a tall husky man who told me he came from Montclair, New Jersey. It turned out he was the Superintendent of Schools. Another lawyer, Walter Rothschild, introduced me to his wife Linda. They lived in Hoboken, New Jersey. Linda, a large, friendly woman, was eager to chat.

"I was born in Germany," she said. "Though I'm not Jewish, I needed to escape the horrible things that were happening. I work in Walter's law firm. You and Don must visit us in Hoboken."

Another couple who lived in Montclair were enthusiastic about the quick commute to NYC and the excellent school system. Except for Linda, none of the women seemed to have jobs outside the home. Joan told me she was a qualified nurse but gave up working when she married Mark. I was an ardent feminist but hesitated to discuss architecture and my new job at the time.

The large ground-floor living space, which flowed into a dining area behind the staircase, was thoughtfully decorated. A blue theme ran through everything, from the sofa cushions to the platters on the carefully laid dining room table, complete with a Waterford glass chandelier.

Drinks, mostly highballs, flowed freely, and aromatic smells of unknown spices wafted from the kitchen. I was starting to feel hungry and munched on some leftover crackers I spied on a side table.

The food, when it came, was an amazing assortment of dishes. There was something for every taste. Not being an accomplished cook, I hesitated to comment, though I was ready to sample everything, realising what I needed was to improve my skills and buy a new cookbook.

When I heard later that Joan was responsible for cooking the dinner, I was duly impressed.

❧•❧

On our way back to Brooklyn, I got the real story from Don.

"You must know about Julia Child – she's all the rage these days."

I nodded in response. I'd browsed through *Mastering the Art of French Cooking*, deciding it was too complex.

"Joan and her good friend Lois wanted to do something for themselves. So, they flew off to France and enrolled in Le Cordon Bleu Paris, each earning a diploma in French cooking. That must have satisfied their egos and added a certain panache to their dinner parties," he laughed. "But remember, Joan is a good friend and most reliable. If you need help or advice, she'll come to the rescue."

❧•❧

We made good use of the rental car over the next few weekends as we looked for a house. Long Island was out because of the long commute, and there was nothing but split-level houses in our price range.

The towns in Westchester County, Larchmont, and White Plains were too expensive. So it was back to New Jersey, and Montclair, with its easy access to the city by train and bus, seemed like the best place to start.

Don had a last-minute idea. "Let's call Sally and Michael Orr. They're old friends from law school days in Minnesota. I visited them several times in the past and liked the feel of the place. They have four kids now and could be looking for a larger house."

Michael Orr gave us the name of the realtor who'd found them their first house – Richard Stanton.

"He's not a hard sell, just a friendly guy with lots of patience. I think you will like him," he told us.

I made an appointment with Dick Stanton for the following weekend.

※·※

Don and I both liked Dick.

We'd been driving around Montclair on our first visit, and I was impressed with the variety of its architecture, from the mansions on the hill to the more modest homes clustered around the railroad stations, of which there are two – one at Watchung Avenue and another in Upper Montclair.

Don needed to be in walking distance of transportation to the city, while I was more concerned about being close to schools and shops. Dick knew our requirements and promised to phone when something turned up.

※·※

Dick showed us more houses the following weekend, but without success. Before we left for the city, Don had an idea.

"How about a fixer-upper?"

I protested with a laugh, imagining myself with a screaming baby on my hip while water dripped from a hole in the roof.

Dick took note of my feelings, but also offered a warning. "If I find anything, be prepared to come out during the week. This town is becoming very popular. Many city dwellers feel the same."

❧⋆❧

Dick was true to his word. A phone call came to my office from Dick's secretary the next morning asking me to take a bus from the Port Authority to Upper Montclair.

"Dick will meet you at the village bus stop," she told me.

At this stage, our baby was due in about six weeks, and I could see clearly that my days in the office were numbered as I struggled up and down the stairs in the subway to get to the Port Authority.

Dick and Don were waiting for me at the bus stop, and we walked together to the house. On our ten-minute walk, Dick talked about the background of the family that lived there at the time.

"The present owners, Peggy Huntington and her mother Mrs Crawley, live in the house, where her family has lived for at least two generations. I know them quite well. Over the years, Peggy fell on hard times and couldn't afford to keep things up. They've just moved to a small apartment, and except for a few bits and pieces, the place is empty."

The house, located at #217 Inwood Avenue, close to the village of Upper Montclair, was one of many vernacular houses built around the turn of the century. Set back about thirty feet from the street, it had no sidewalk. A huge oak tree defined the front lawn. A flagstone path led to a flight of steps with wrought-iron railings leading up to the door. The panelled entrance door had sidelights and a decorative fanlight. I was aware it had been altered – the front porch moved to the back and a floor-length multilight window inserted at the centre of the front elevation, but I wasn't too bothered about the alterations and was very excited to see the interior.

Making a mental note not to focus on what might have been, I decided to look at the possibilities. Yes, the living room had a hole in the ceiling, but the large spaces, bay windows, and traditional mouldings created a bright, friendly interior. Don loved the large open fireplace. Removing the doors between the original parlours had created a more open space that flowed gracefully from the open-hall stairway to the large dining area and kitchen at the back. Don was more interested in replanning the kitchen.

"I need to see the basement and look at the foundations and heating system. Why don't you check out the upper floors?"

I found four moderate-sized bedrooms upstairs, the largest of which had a working fireplace. There were also two bathrooms that needed refitting. The two attic rooms facing the street had possibilities, but that was an issue for another time.

After lunch in the village, we weighed the options. House-hunting had worn us both out. Don was happy with the commute. I was excited about the house and the convenient distance from the village.

We decided to make an offer based on the building inspection.

It was back to work after that. After almost a week of anxiety, Dick Stanton called with news that the offer had been accepted and we could move in whenever it was convenient.

✦·✦

The office gave me a big send off with an afternoon party to a background of the Beatles' music. Gus and Peggy promised to visit us in Montclair.

The move went smoothly, and the neighbours seemed friendly. A lovely woman across the street called by the day after we arrived. She was beautiful with flawless skin and friendly blue eyes.

"I'm Madeline Murphy," she said by way of introduction. "My husband and I came here from Newfoundland about ten years ago. Montclair is a great place to live, though I haven't had much chance to explore what's going on." She took note of the fact that I was expecting a baby and continued, "We have six children, and I know one of my girls would love to babysit when the time comes."

We chose a room for the baby, and Don painted it bright yellow. I ordered a crib and other necessary things from the Sears catalogue. I knew nothing about babies, though Don and I took Elisabeth Bing's natural childbirth classes, a trendy thing to do at the time.

I bought a copy of Doctor Spock's *The Common Sense Book of Baby and Child Care*. Don, who knew much more than I did because of his large family, thought it was a load of rubbish.

The baby, a boy, was born without much ado at St. Vincent's hospital in New York City on September 19, 1968. Ms Bing's classes helped with the labour, though I needed an epidural at the end.

We named him John McArevey after my paternal grandfather. He was baptised by Father Edward Larkin at St. Cassian's church in Montclair. My sister Esmay and her husband Michael Rothschild from Dublin were the godparents.

Our house on Inwood Avenue in Montclair.

MONTCLAIR, NEW JERSEY: CHILDREN AND THE SUBURBS

After the nurse left, we settled into some sort of routine. Don took an early morning bus to the city, which left from the top of the street, and I was left to the demands of the new baby. I was grateful for the time alone, and there was plenty of diversion. A handyman recommended by Dick came to fix the hole in the living room ceiling, and a chimney sweep inspected the fireplace flue.

A blaze of autumn sunshine lit up the sparsely furnished interior. Smells of decayed foliage and loamy earth wafted through the open window.

I was mindful of the need to get some extra furniture, though it was more important to draw plans for the combined kitchen and laundry room. What I really needed, however, was to get out of the house and explore the village.

What was left of the leaves swirled in the morning breeze when I set out to the top of Valley Road to check out the grocery store with John in a baby sling. On the next block, I noticed a pharmacy and hardware store. A tall woman in jogging shorts waved to John. The air smelled of coffee and fall. An impressive, steeply gabled, gothic-revival church defined the south-east corner of a busy intersecting street. Crossing Valley Road and walking past a movie house, I headed to the railroad station and crossed the tracks where a group of feral cats was happily feeding in a concealed hollow. Careful not to disturb them, I proceeded to a moderate-sized park with a path for joggers and dog-walkers. A man was playing ball with a puppy on the ball field. I found a bench and sat to observe their fun.

John, ever hungry, began to whimper. *Maybe it's time to return to Inwood Avenue.*

❧

Walking home, I felt a sense of confidence and peace. *Whatever the future brings, this town is where we belong.*

John was a happy and friendly child, but he demanded attention. I'd learnt to ignore the messy house and set up my drawing board in one of the empty bedrooms to sketch plans for our new kitchen and work when he napped.

❧

By mid-fall, it was still warm out. With John on my back this time, I strolled up to the village to find the library and check out what was playing at the movie theatre. After I returned home, Sally Orr called.

"I remember you asking about someone to play tennis with," she said. "Maybe you're ready for a game. I have friends that often need an extra player. Let me know if you are interested."

I agreed, feeling healthy and well. John was gaining weight and almost totally on solid food by that point. I'd almost forgotten when I'd last played – maybe on the public courts in Central Park – but I felt running around might do me good. Don agreed, and I searched the attic dump room for my racquet.

In a matter of days, Sally's friend, Connie Duhamel, a tall friendly woman with freckles and a frizzy hairdo, picked me up. We drove to the Montclair Country Club, an impressive building on the top of the hill, close to the Verona border. Sally's friend was eager to chat about Montclair and her family.

"My youngest daughter is a year older than your John. I have seven daughters. Tennis helps me to survive. I hope you have some reliable babysitters."

I couldn't imagine having so many children but hesitated to mention the Pill. Besides, she might have wanted that many!

We played vigorous tennis for about an hour. Then, suddenly and for no apparent reason, my right leg collapsed, and I was flat on the ground. The next thing I remembered, I was on a gurney with a pretty nurse holding my hand.

"Don't worry, you're going for an X-ray," she reassured me. "I've given you an injection so you shouldn't be in pain."

❦

I'd broken my Achilles tendon.

The same nurse came to see me after the X-ray.

"The surgeon will be with you shortly," she said. "A member of your tennis group notified your husband. By now he should be on his way back to Montclair."

I breathed a sigh of relief knowing Madeline Murphy or one of her girls was taking care of John.

After a long wait, the doctor arrived. A taciturn man of few words, he looked carefully at my ankle and made an assessment before I was taken through for surgery.

❧·❧

I was completely out during the operation and returned to consciousness slowly.

"You will be in a plaster cast for at least two months and unable to move around without crutches," the doctor told me. "Make an appointment to see me next month."

Without a glance in my direction, he was out the door. It seemed like a bad dream, and I was feeling angry and depressed. Don arrived soon after, and we drove back to Inwood Avenue. Despite the injection, my leg felt sore and uncomfortable. Don was sympathetic but practical.

"I will hire someone to take care of you and the baby," he said. "One of the Murphy girls can help out until she arrives, and I'll be available at the weekends."

We also bought a television, which I was told was essential with live-in helpers, though I still used the public radio station for news of the outside world.

Olga Pettersen, a tall Swedish woman with grey eyes and a slight accent, arrived the following Monday. John whined at first, but they quickly became friends.

"I'm used to babies," she said to me. "My daughter has two girls, now in middle school. I came from Sweden to take care of them when my husband passed."

Besides keeping John happy and taking him for walks in a new stroller, Olga was a good cook and loved to bake, a blessing for me since I'd had no interest in cooking since we'd moved in and doubted I would before we had our new kitchen.

On Friday evenings, we dropped Olga at her daughter's house, thirty minutes away in a small town off the Parkway. Getting through this period was a challenge, as I had to learn to manipulate the stairs on my butt and hop around the first floor, since we'd installed a carpet in the open living space.

❈•❈

To cheer me up, Don decided to have a party. Without a word to me, he contacted our good friend Joan Frawley from White Plains. She arrived one weekend with balloons, streamers, and snacks, as well as a pair of glamorous silk trousers that would cover the cast on my leg.

Don's friends from Hoboken and a few from out of town dropped by as well, and Sally Orr brought additional goodies. Our new neighbours John and Madeline Murphy were there as well. Everyone had a good time. I felt more cheerful and started thinking of imaginative ways to keep me sane till my leg healed.

It was late fall, and I yearned for the outdoors.

❈•❈

After school, when the babysitter arrived, I sat pulling weeds on the front lawn or reading in a beach chair. I'd finished Tolstoy's *War and Peace* before they removed the plaster from my right leg.

Neighbours dropped in for a chat. It was almost like being back in the real world. To make sure I could truly walk safely, we kept Olga around for an extra week.

❧•❧

This was around the time of the Space Race, and the news of the impending moon landing was everywhere. It was set to take place at the end of the week. Joan Chang, a new friend who lived up the street, asked if I wanted to watch the show at her house.

"We have a new wide screen, and my husband is out of town. I'd love for you to join me," she said.

Since Don was quite happy taking care of John and was content to watch the event on our smaller screen, I agreed to join her. The evening was a memorable one, since not only was it the first time anyone had been on the moon, but also because Buzz Aldrin grew up in a house near Anderson Park (not far from our house) where I used to walk John.

I got to know my hostess during the broadcast. A tall, elegant middle-aged woman and former ballet dancer, Joan was thinking of returning to work as an administrator in the theatrical world. She was trying to find something in Montclair, but so far wasn't having any luck.

❧•❧

To meet new friends and broaden my outlook, I joined the Montclair Adult School, which met at the Montclair public library. Though most of the courses focused on practical skills, on Fridays they had a guest speaker from one of NYC's universities or art institutions speak on current events. I decided to volunteer, though I wasn't sure where I could be of use.

Meanwhile, the house badly needed extra furniture, preferably vintage. What I had was Danish modern and totally inappropriate for a Victorian house. We also had no table to fill our large dining room. Madeline Murphy suggested I visit used furniture sales every Saturday in Clifton, an adjoining suburb. As luck would it have it, I found an elegant table with an extra leaf and eight matching chairs at a modest price.

❖

The kitchen/laundry and toilet complex were almost finished, and Don thought we should have a dinner party. Madeline and John Murphy were our first guests. It was early fall and still warm. A gentle breeze drifted in through the slightly open windows. John was safely in bed, and I had a baby monitor in case he cried out.

When they arrived, Madeline was as beautiful as ever in a fancy silk dress, and John was the same handsome, brown-eyed man; he was wearing a blazer and well-tailored slacks.

Don greeted them at the door. "At last, I have a chance to meet you. Madeline has been so helpful to Eleanor. Let's have a drink before dinner. We have enough chairs for everyone now."

Over my version of Boeuf Bourguignon and veggies, we asked them about Newfoundland, which I knew little about. Luckily, John was eager to talk about it. I noticed the trace of an English accent in his voice.

"Madeline's ancestors came from Ireland, way back in the time of the Famine, and are now part of the establishment. My family has ties to England and arrived later. I was sent to a fancy public school in Yorkshire, which looking back, was a mistake. A fancy prep school education doesn't stand for much when you're looking for a job in the US or Canada, where a college education is almost mandatory. Twenty years ago, the UK was in recession, and we were forced to immigrate, but I'm heartened that my kids are good students and ambitious to succeed."

Despite these disadvantages, John had an intelligent, understated sense of humour entertaining us with amusing stories of this wild and desolate island.

After they left, Don, who came from a poor mid-western family, realised how lucky he was to have had a college education, allowing him to have a successful career. It struck me suddenly how quickly time had passed – it seemed like we had hosted the party after I broke my Achilles tendon just yesterday, though in reality almost two years had passed.

❧•❧

I continued walking around the neighbourhood with John, which enabled me to dismiss all the negative thoughts I'd held about suburban living. Compared to Europe, where houses and gardens were hidden behind walls and high fences, Americans were open and friendly. They liked to show off their houses, admire the plants and flowers, and even comment on the architecture.

❧❧

Winter came quickly, and our archaic heating system chugged away keeping us warm. One night, while John was safely in bed, Don lit a fire in the open fireplace. He took the opportunity to urge me to buy a screen.

While most of the heat went up the chimney, having a fire created a feeling of comfort and order. The old house smelled of pinewood and apples. I was stretched out on the couch with Harper Lee's *To Kill a Mockingbird*. Don gazed at the fire with a gin and tonic and took a brief detour into the past.

"When I lived in Litchfield with my grandmother, a school friend and single child would often ask me back for supper," he began. "His father was the local lawyer and would always light a fire and stand on the Persian rug warming his hands. I remember thinking that if I was ever rich enough to own a house, I would do the same. Maybe now is the time to buy that Persian rug?"

He looked back at me with a smile.

I was pregnant again, and Don was delighted. I'd checked with doctor, and so far, all was well.

"Why don't we take John to Ireland in the summer? When we have two children, it won't be so easy. Mummy will be delighted – finally another male grandchild to spoil after so many girls."

And so, it was settled.

❧❧

Before we left for Ireland, I got a driver's licence and bought a car seat.

We left from JFK for Dublin in July. John was a restive child, and we didn't get much sleep on the overnight flight. I felt slightly nauseous, but a strong cup of tea and some biscuits at the airport got us through customs. The cool Irish air was a welcome relief after a sweltering New Jersey summer.

We stayed with Mummy and Aunty Daisy in their small modern house on Hyde Road, close to Esmay and Michael's on Elton Park.

Mummy spoiled John, bought him fancy outfits, and called him 'my little prince'. He was a very social child and responded well.

❧•❧

With someone always available to take care of John, I felt free to see some old friends, especially Mary King, my buddy from my San Francisco days.

We strolled along the Dún Laoghaire pier on a bright summer day while waves lapped gently against the granite wall. The air smelled of ozone and kelp. Casually dressed in cut-offs and a striped cotton sweater, Mary was unusually silent. Time passed, and I commented on the marine activity in the harbour. Then, totally unprompted, she decided to unwind.

"I have no regrets and sometimes miss those golden years, but Dublin is home now. I inherited some money and built a small house in Sandymount. I'm still working for Bord Failte. The job is terrific. I oversee the design and furnishings of Irish Embassies in Europe, which puts me in touch with the local culture and improves my language skills."

Her expression changed. "But life is full of unpleasant surprises. I was diagnosed with breast cancer a month ago. Fortunately, it's not the invasive type and can be treated externally."

I put my arms around her, and we cried together.

We reached the lighthouse at the end of the pier, climbed up to top level, and turned to look back at the familiar view of church spires, Victorian hotels, small cottages, and yacht clubs that lined the waterfront. I felt an odd sense of belonging, even though this was no longer my home.

"Let's walk back and snag a drink at Esmay and Michael's," I said.

Mary replied, "I'd love to, but I have a theatre date this evening and need to shower and change. Let's touch base before you leave."

We hugged before heading our separate ways – Mary to drive her car to Sandymount, and I to walk back to Hyde Road.

A NEW ADDITION TO THE FAMILY

A week later, Don and I were back in Montclair dealing with what remained of a hot summer. A noisy attic fan helped to cool the house. John cooled off by splashing around in a plastic pool in the backyard.

We ate on the back porch now. I bought white-painted Victorian furniture at a local auction and adopted a beautiful orange cat with green eyes called Wozzie from the local shelter. John loved the animal, the first of many pets he acquired over time.

An ultrasound at the local hospital confirmed that all was well, and that the baby was a girl. We were both delighted and decided to wallpaper her bedroom, since the old lath and plaster walls were uneven.

Planning for the future, I discovered a day-care centre for preschool-aged children in a Presbyterian church at the other end of Inwood Avenue.

❧•❧

Margaret McArevey Price was born on November 28, 1970, and named after Aunty Daisy, my second mother and mentor. This time the Lamaze method really worked. My labour was quick and almost painless. We returned to Montclair from St. Vincent's Hospital in NYC on a freezing day.

John stayed overnight at the Murphy house. Margaret was an easy baby and took to breastfeeding. Don was able to take a few days off to take care of John, who was madly jealous of his new sister. The first time we took him in to see her, he threw his teddy bear in her face and left. There was no apparent damage to the baby.

I was totally exhausted, but Don took charge. He put John in his crib with the new cat and read them both a story. After a while, my energy returned.

By this time, I had a new next-door neighbour with three children. Jimmy, the youngest, was the same age as John. His mother was delighted.

"John is welcome to come over to play. My other children are much older and have their own friends, but Jimmy will welcome the company."

❧❧

A few days later, baby Margaret was baptised at St. Cassian's, the local church, by Father Edward Larkin. Madeline and John Murphy stood in for the godparents, Mary King, who was in Dublin, and my cousin Patrick O'Keefe, who was out of the country. I remember a freezing day, a roaring fire, and hot toddies.

After the baptism, I fed Margaret, who had calmly survived all the attention. Fortunately, John was staying overnight with his new friend next door.

Aunty Daisy and Mummy called with congratulations. Aunty Daisy then took the phone.

"I've always wanted to visit the United States, especially New York City," she said. "Now I have an excuse and plan to do so. Let me know a convenient time."

Don was delighted. He loved Aunty Daisy, and there was nothing he liked better than showing visitors the sights of NYC. With the festive season almost upon us, Aunty Daisy agreed to wait until spring.

❧❧

Aunty Daisy arrived with the cherry blossoms in the nearby Branch Brook Park. Don met her at the airport. She was now a tallish older woman of fair complexion in a lined raincoat, with sensible walking shoes and a jaunty felt hat.

I stayed at home with the kids. John, these days a boisterous and chatty two year old, was excited. He remembered Aunty Di from our visit to Dublin. Margaret, almost six months old by then, viewed the world with wonder and curiosity.

After dinner, when the kids were in bed, we talked and made plans for the time she would be with us. Daisy agreed to whatever we came up with; her only stipulations were that we visit the Metropolitan Museum and walk around Greenwich Village.

❧❧

Since the weather forecast predicted sunshine, our first trip was to take the Circle Line, which the kids enjoyed

281

as much as Aunty Daisy. I remembered taking the same trip with Cousin Roddy when I first arrived in the States. During the week, when John was at day-care, we walked around Upper Montclair Village, me with Margaret on my back.

On another day, I took Daisy to Crane House, home of the Montclair Historical Society. Daisy was fascinated by the many parks and by the use of wood in suburban architecture – so different from the concrete-and-brick exteriors of suburban housing in Ireland and elsewhere in Britain.

Another weekend in NYC, we visited the Metropolitan, Frick, and MOMA Museums. Though very much a traditionalist, Daisy was intrigued by Gauguin and Van Gogh. During that week, I also arranged for the two of us to have lunch with my old friend Yvonne Westfried, who was still living on Park Avenue in Manhattan.

Her husband had unfortunately passed away some years ago, but Yvonne was as sprightly as ever recalling stories of living in Paris during the war.

⚜

The highlight of Aunty Daisy's trip was a visit to Sotheby's Auction House followed by afternoon tea at the Plaza.

I was sad to say goodbye to this strong, multi-talented woman, who not only supported my mother and my siblings, but also guided the rest of her large family through the influenza epidemic of 1918 and the horrors of two world wars.

GRADUATE SCHOOL, AND A NEW CAREER

John was now in second grade, and Margaret would be starting first grade in the fall. They walked along Valley Road to our neighbourhood school. Women's liberation was very much in the air. Gloria Steinem was set to speak in Montclair next month.

We also had new neighbours, Joan and Michael Gordon, a Jewish family with three children. The youngest Gordon daughter, Stephanie, and Margaret became friends. The Gordons' older children, Eric and Samantha, were at the high school. Joan, a youthful looking mom with curly black hair and twinkling brown eyes was eager to chat. They had just moved from Baltimore.

"I'm having a consciousness-raising party next week and would love you to join us. I'm a yoga fanatic," she said to me one day.

Don was amused. "Why not? It might be fun. You never know who might be there."

.

I was also curious, though somewhat sceptical, having been to such parties in Brooklyn Heights and New York City.

❧

To my surprise, the party was friendly and lots of fun, with an interesting mix of women, some from nearby towns and others from the neighbourhood. Many had gone to college and married early, while a few were divorced.

With their kids almost grown, their main complaint was boredom. We all agreed to meet at Gloria Steinem's talk and arranged to get together again to discuss it afterwards.

I wasn't enthusiastic about going back to the drawing board and was either too reluctant or too lazy to learn CAD, the new software for design projects, but I needed to explore what was available to me with my architectural background.

With this in mind, I joined a bus tour organised by the Montclair Historical Society to Fraunces Tavern in New York City. I knew nothing about the site, except that it was one of the oldest buildings in the city with connections to the Revolutionary War and George Washington.

A cheerful young woman in colonial attire welcomed us to the site and gave a detailed account of its historic significance. She was more than happy to answer questions.

After coffee and cookies provided by the staff, she gave us a tour of the building, explaining early construction practices from splicing timber beams to preventing dampness, since the building was located close to the seaport. At the end of the day, I congratulated her on how well she led the tour.

"I'm completing my first year of a degree in historic preservation at Columbia University. It's a fabulous program, most of the students are older with degrees in architecture and history," she told me.

Don understood my interest in returning to work and suggested I find out about the program. "With your credentials and background working in NYC and California, you should have an edge."

I wasn't so sure, but I sent for the papers anyway.

After completing the various forms and an interview with the Dean, I was accepted into the program, which started in September.

With respect to the kids' schedule, it would be fine. John had sports practice every afternoon, and Margaret and Stephanie Gordon, now close friends, continued to walk home together in the afternoons. For later classes, I would organise a sitter. It all seemed too good to be true.

❖•❖

That summer was warmer than usual. I took the kids to the public pool up the hill near the Iris Gardens. Connie Duhamel wanted us to join the Montclair Golf Club, which had an Olympic-style pool, but Don would have none of it.

My good friend Barbara Hippel, from San Francisco days, now married and living in in the area, told me about Deer Lake, a less pretentious club about a half hour's drive from Montclair. I was, however, puzzled by their strange admission process: a tea party without refreshments or tea.

Don was suspicious, but let it go. Barbara and I were already planning a trip there for the next weekend, and I would take Joan and Stephanie Gordon with me another time.

Deer Lake was a casual place with good swimming and a modest clubhouse. I could see a few water slides and row boats to hire. They also had a lifeguard. But I couldn't see anyone from Montclair.

Out of curiosity, Don came along one evening after work.

"While it's pleasantly casual, there's something odd about the place. I see a few young men floating around cleaning the clubhouse and bathroom facilities, but no one seems to be in charge."

After a few weeks, Joan Gordon asked me to propose her family for membership. We filled out the forms and received a date for the tealess tea. Our two families attended together; everyone was polite, but there was no chitchat. Not long afterwards, a carefully worded letter informed us that the Gordons' request for membership had been denied. Don was furious.

"Blatant antisemitism. We should resign our membership."

Although we were upset by the antisemitism of the club, I am embarrassed to say that we didn't leave at that time.

❧•❧

My classes at Columbia began in September. Margaret and John were back at school by then.

The commute by bus and subway worked well and gave me plenty of time to study. I was curious and excited. Professor James Marsden Fitch, who started the program, gave an introductory speech.

It was a five-day week, with most of the classes taking place in the morning. This was fine, though I do remember feeling nervous on a particular afternoon class when I needed to bring the children with me. Fortunately, that worry was unfounded. With promises of sandwiches at Chock-Full-of Nuts and ice cream afterwards, they sat quietly through a lecture about ancient plumbing practices in the US and Britain.

❧

By then, I had a more serious concern. Don had been offered a job as the lawyer for a small venture capital company and decided to leave his job at the New York law firm.

"I need a change, and I've always wanted to try venture capital. The job entails longer working hours and trips to other cities and sometimes abroad. Let's see how it works out."

I supported his decision, but with reservations. He was looking more tired than usual, which made me worry about his health and the effect of long-distance travel.

❧

Meanwhile, I was still enjoying my time at Columbia – the research and visiting historic sites where my architectural experience could be put to good use made me happy. Don followed my work with interest when he wasn't travelling and made a point to come to my graduation.

"Your next challenge is how to decide the best way to use all this new information without leaving Montclair," he laughed.

I agreed and actually had an idea of how I might do just that, but it needed research.

The Montclair Historical Society had attempted to record its vast collection of historic houses and sites, but without much success. I wanted to make a comprehensive inventory of the architecture in the town and presented the idea at the next board meeting. I was encouraged by their enthusiasm, but also a little apprehensive. *What have I let myself in for?*

"We will need volunteers to help with photography, research in local libraries and other stuff. We'll also need funding from local organisations, a place to meet and the approval of the State Preservation office in Trenton."

Coverage in the press and on the local radio station brought volunteers, and the Church of St. Luke in downtown Montclair offered us a basement room to meet in. We also received a large cheque from the Junior League of Montclair, which helped with expenses.

One of my most enthusiastic volunteers, Mary Delaney Krugman, a lawyer and stay-at-home mother, helped me launch the project, which took almost a year to complete.

The State Preservation Office was impressed by our work and suggested we extend it across the town by dividing it into a number of Historic Districts.

Once again, we attracted additional volunteers with research experience in history and architecture. Maynette Breithaupt, a new arrival in Montclair from Austin, Texas, became my good friend and assistant. She was familiar with the process and loved research. The Newark Public Library, as well as our own local library, provided a wealth of information.

BLOCK ISLAND

During the summers when we didn't visit Ireland or Minnesota, we stayed in the Cutting Cottages on Block Island, a short ferry ride from Point Judith in Rhode Island.

Jim and Ruth Levitan, old friends of Don's from their early law firm days, had recommended the cottages, which they had visited some years ago with their children. They had liked the casual atmosphere.

Mrs Cutting, a widow from South Carolina, had bought the land as an investment in the 1960s and built twenty small cottages around a sports field on a high bluff facing Mansion Beach on the Island's east side. She spent her summers there and returned south for the winter.

The modest wood-framed buildings with their brightly painted doors provided accommodation for an average-sized family. They smelled of camphor carbolic soap.

The restrictions were loose, though once a day Mrs Cutting would ride around the compound in her old rattletrap Ford, checking the area for untoward goings-on. On our first visit, she introduced herself, making sure everything was in order. It was clear the steely look behind the smile was not to be trifled with.

❧•❧

Don fell in love with the place, as did the children, who usually each brought along a friend. He would take the boys fishing in one of the many ponds. I was enchanted. The stone walls, narrow roads, and bleak landscape reminded me of Ireland.

Margaret and a few other little girls formed a play group in the compound, which left me free to read and explore the Island on my bike with Ruth Levitan, with whom I eventually developed a long-term friendship. Though we came from very different backgrounds, we had much in common: literature, politics, and gardens. She grew up in the toxic political environment of life post World War II. Ruth's father, Harry Dexter White, was an official with the United States Department of the Treasury and an important figure in the 1948 Bretton Woods Conference.[1]

I knew little about American politics at the time, though I was aware of international espionage from stories in the *New York Times* and my love of detective fiction.

❧•❧

---

[1] *Harry White (Ruth Levitan's father) was the major architect of the International Monetary Fund. In 1948, he was accused of spying for the Soviet Union, which he adamantly denied. He was never a member of the Communist Party.*

During our later years on Block Island, when the bluefish were running, Don and Jim Levitan disappeared for the day and returned with more than we could eat. There was no concept of 'waste not, want not'. It took years for me to enjoy eating blue fish again.

We had our treats as well. Once a week, we got all dressed up and went out to dinner at the Spring House Inn.

❖

One warm summer morning, I was reading *Watership Down* in the long meadow grass imagining I was down there with the rabbits. Returning to lunch I found Don glued to the radio.

"Daniel Berrigan, the anti-war Jesuit priest activist, who was part of the Catonsville Nine and burnt the draft records of the Vietnam War, is seeking refuge at the house of the Reverend William Stringfellow, an Episcopal priest on Block Island," said the voice of the newscaster.

Don mentioned that he thought the Island was an easy place to disappear, but I wasn't so sure. The story did create a sense of excitement among the residents of Cutting Cottages. Berrigan was eventually arrested posing as a bird watcher in a barn close to the Stringfellow residence.

Starting in 1989, there was a wave of 'tearing down' on the Island, including the demolition of the Cutting Cottages to make space for townhouses.

❖

Before we retired to Wilmington, North Carolina, we visited these new townhouses on Block Island with the Levitans. They were comfortable and equipped with modern conveniences, but they would never be the same as the Cutting Cottages.

MEDICAL PROBLEMS, AND
MY SHORT-LIVED REAL ESTATE CAREER

Meanwhile, my children were growing, doing well at school, and developing their own interests. Margaret, a loner, preferred swimming and bike riding, while John, who excelled at lacrosse, was offered a scholarship to attend the University of Pennsylvania. But life isn't always fair, and an injury to one of his legs resulted in a diagnosis of ankylosing spondylitis.

This hereditary disease typically attacks young men in the age range of 17–35, and a DNA test revealed the defective gene came from Don's maternal family. I wept silent tears at the news.

And that wasn't the only medical issue we had to contend with. Though he had an exciting new job with the Equitable Insurance Company, Don was becoming increasingly more exhausted – worryingly so. It was concerning enough that he sought out medical advice, and a heart specialist at New York Hospital recommended open-heart surgery.

The operation was successful, but Don was told he needed to stay a while longer in the hospital.

I talked with the surgeon afterwards, who briefed me on home care.

"The key to a full recovery is daily exercise, no matter how painful, increasing the distance every day," were the instructions.

Starting this regime in the hospital, Don was grumpy and full of complaints, but I could see the colour returning to his cheeks. As we walked along the hospital corridors, I could feel him wince with every step. And then it was time to go home.

Back in Montclair, it felt like winter. We assumed a strict routine, walking in the neighbourhood every day and later venturing to the local mall.

Don's good spirits returned. Friends from NYC came out to visit, and I put my work on hold. We relaxed and enjoyed new friends and driving to nearby towns in search of good restaurants.

Mike and Sally Orr, Don's old friends from Minnesota, invited us for Christmas dinner, as they had done every year since we moved to Montclair. Their older children were home from their various colleges.

Don was feeling much better by that time and was eager to return to work. He decided to drive rather than take public transportation.

Things were flowing at their own pace. Don would come home early for dinner and putter around in the back garden. Overseas visitors came to stay. Many political changes took place overseas, like the fall of the Berlin Wall and Reagan and Gorbachev working to end the

Cold War. Prime Minister Margaret Thatcher supported Reagan's conservative policies.

Don would often shake his head and was looking forward to retirement.

"I'd love to live in a warmer climate. I'm fed up with commuting," he would say.

Thinking of the children's college fees, I felt I should contribute. My preservation work for the Historical Society was fascinating, but not remunerative. By the following year, most of the Historic Districts would be submitted to the State Office for approval, so it was a good time to consider making a career change.

With my knowledge of Montclair's architecture, real estate seemed like a good choice, and I enjoyed matching buyers and houses. Closing the deal was another matter.

Because of my architectural background, I got a few high-priced listings that paid off. But I disliked the cut-throat nature of the business, the constant phone calls and messages. I became nervous and lost sleep. Don suggested I give it up, which I eventually did, having made a good chunk of money.

❧•❧

Despite the ups and downs of my real estate venture, I won't easily forget my last deal.

I had just listed and sold one of the town's oldest properties on Union Street to the rector of St. Luke's, the town's most important Episcopal church, and his wife, who was also the financial advisor to the church on a national level.

The deal went through, and I received a hefty financial payment, which I was delighted and pleased about.

However, about a week later at breakfast, Don was reading *The Montclair Times* and called out to me. "Listen to this," he said, and began reading from the newspaper.

> *Wife of prominent Episcopal rector arrested for fraud and larceny. It appears she was also financial advisor to the national church and a local shoplifter.*

"At least you got paid," he said, and we both had a good laugh. It was time to put real estate behind me.

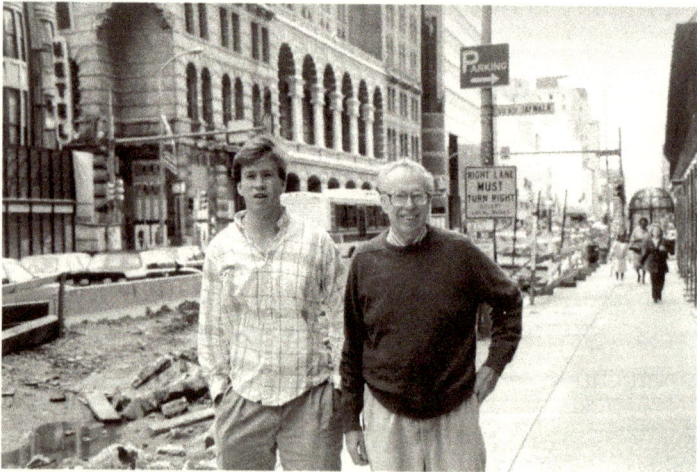

John and Don in Philadelphia, circa 1987.

AT WORK WITH A WOMAN OF SOME IMPORTANCE

Eleanore Pettersen stood in her office, arranging the workday with Dave Rinaldi, her project overseer. She was large, blonde, and imperious, with an ample bosom and wonderful posture. She was also the first female architect to graduate from Cooper Union in New York City.

She had made it to the top, where women feared to tread at that time, and was quick to remind everyone of her importance.

I sometimes imagined the conversation she was having the day I was hired.

It was likely about Henry Duckworth, who planned to create condominiums in an abandoned church in Hoboken. He might have suggested extra help, preferably from someone who knew about historic buildings.

She would then have told Dave, her office manager, about it.

"So, I've called Eleanor Price, a preservation planner in Montclair," she might have said. "She's interested and will drop by about 2:30pm. Show her around, will you, if I am delayed? And just keep an eye on things and put the dogs outside. I'll be out until about 3pm."

❖•❖

Somewhat bored with documenting historic buildings at this point, I welcomed Eleanore Petterson's call. It was a chance to do proper preservation, and I felt excited about this new adventure.*

Not wearing a coat on that warm day, I found myself driving my old Beetle through Saddle River, a posh suburb in New Jersey with large widely spaced homes often concealed behind gates or groves of trees, which was a stark contrast to the generally overcrowded New Jersey. *An area reeking of wealth and anonymity!*

My instructions were to look for a hanging sign in a grove of trees on the north side of Fernwood Avenue. As I searched for the sign, I found myself wondering whether her clients would have the patience necessary to find it. Eventually, I found her sign on the post of a small wrought-iron gate, which in turn was attached to a fence along the property line.

Opening the creaking gate, I followed a narrow flagstone path to the converted barn that housed Eleanore's office. Sunshine danced along the weathered

---

*I think I worked for Eleanore Petterson before I sold real estate. Consequently, the earlier mention of going straight from historic preservation to real estate is incorrect.

barn shingles, and two dogs ran around happily in the untamed garden. The air smelled of earth and decaying plants.

I was welcomed by Dave; Eleanore was still out. He began his tour of the barn in a managerial tone, which I later learned was not his usual style.

"Where would I work?" I asked him, surveying the platforms above me and the flimsy stairs connecting them.

"We could fit you in on the second platform. I work on the first floor where Miss Pettersen has her office and conference room."

I could feel my phobia about heights making itself known, but I managed to play it cool and decided to discuss the prospect with Eleanore. Just then, our quiet tour was halted by the loud screech of brakes outside.

"Okay gang, back to your drawing boards! Here comes Miss Pettersen," Dave called to the young men on the levels above us, gesturing me into the conference room.

In a matter of seconds, Eleanore swished into the barn, a black pashmina draped around her neck, followed by her two dogs, Georgette and Chang. She appeared to be in a jovial mood, addressing us both, waving to her interns, and petting the animals.

"I hope you showed Eleanor around, Dave, and introduced her to the staff. I've just had a successful lunch with our local congressman. After two martinis, I convinced him he should change the zoning along the river for our proposed condos. But we'll discuss that later. Right now, I must talk with Eleanor."

Without further ado, she swept me into her office and closed the door.

The conference area was small with just enough space for a large drawing table, two chairs, and a little desk. Photographs of buildings in various stages of construction lined the walls. The rest of the room was an interesting clutter of papers, drawings, and crawling plants.

Uneasy about a commitment, I suggested I'd like to begin work as a consultant.

As I drove home, I concluded that, behind all the bluff and bluster, Eleanore was really a nice person.

I settled in to work at the unusual building. From a decrepit barn on an acre of land, Eleanore had created an open, multi-level workspace as well as an apartment for herself and a tenant at the back of the property. Its high ceiling and uncluttered space allowed for three platforms to be cantilevered from the walls at different levels, providing space for at least two drafting boards, plan chests, and other necessary equipment. Open stairways connected the platforms to each other. Clients adored the space, which wasn't as functional as it looked. The stairs were too narrow, which made them difficult to navigate, and the acoustics were poor, but as Eleanore told the staff on occasion, even Mr Wright's buildings had their problems. She herself had worked as an apprentice to Frank Lloyd Wright in Taliesin and still regarded him as her mentor.

On our road trips to Hoboken, she would regale me with stories of him and reminisce about her young life as a daring young female architect. Whenever I arrived at our meeting place, she would already be inside the car, a vintage mustard Mercedes, gunning the motor, impatient to leave, wrapped in a black fur-lined cloak. In a matter of minutes, we would be roaring down the Parkway at breakneck speed. I enjoyed these frequent jaunts across the state to Hoboken.

"I love driving," she declared during one such trip. "My father allowed me to drive a truck when I was sixteen, which came in useful when I went to work with Mr Wright in New Mexico. I was one of the only students with a driving license."

Then, she would begin a diatribe about her days at Taliesin and the demands of Mr Wright, whom she considered vain and arrogant.

"Mr Wright was self-conscious about being short. Even the cars on his drawings were small. I never wore high-heeled shoes in his presence."

Luckily, she could rise above any challenges, even to the point of covering up one personal affliction: narcolepsy, which could cause her to drift off without notice at any moment.

"If I ever start looking sleepy, you must order me to stop and wake up!" she laughed.

Dave was certainly right when he warned me about Eleanore's wild driving. But since everything about her was equally dramatic, I filed this information away as just another facet of this unique woman. She could charm you with a smile or wither you with a frosty glance. Builders jumped to attention when she appeared on a site. Clients listened in amazement as she presented her plans.

❧❧

One afternoon in the car, I noticed my companion's face looked white and drawn. She had stopped talking. I was horrified. It suddenly dawned on me that I might have to co-pilot the Mercedes from the passenger seat. There would be no possibility of stopping the car on the section of the highway that we were on, just past the Meadowlands. Grabbing the wheel from this angle would be out of the question. Waking her suddenly might be even worse. I said a fast prayer and loudly suggested we take the upcoming exit, which went through Jersey City. That route would allow us to stop and turn into a side street.

Eleanore's eyes were starting to close tightly as we approached the end of the ramp feeding onto Kennedy Boulevard. Behind us, the traffic suddenly slowed down. I slid over on the seat, snatched the right side of the steering wheel with my left hand and began to feel for the brake pedal with my left foot. My companion blissfully slumped away from me and against the driver's-side door, forcing me to make a sharp turn into the guardrail. The mustard Mercedes shuddered and stopped. Brakes screeched behind us as cars piled up. Everything came to a standstill.

Stunned by the impact, I realised that Eleanore was still fast asleep. A man from the car behind approached us and tried to open the door, which was badly twisted.

"I'll stay here until the police arrive," he said to me. "It's a bad rear-ender. You're lucky not to have been killed."

By the time the police arrived, Eleanore was starting to wake up. I explained to her that I was forced to grab the wheel and save us from a much worse disaster. She was most solicitous and confused. The police took all the information and suggested we check into the local hospital. Despite a wrecked bumper and large dents to the trunk, the car could still be driven. A friendly doctor pronounced us totally fit but recommended that Eleanore never drive alone on the highway and should consider hiring a driver.

Eleanore was unfazed. She turned to me and said, "Let's have lunch."

By that time, I was cold, hungry and extremely tired. After a hot whiskey and pastrami sandwiches at the Captain's Table in Jersey City, we agreed to abandon the Hoboken trip for another day.

❧

Eleanore never did hire a driver, but rarely drove alone on crowded highways after that. I worked at the firm for two years, coming to love the space – the way the light streamed through the east windows casting shadows on the quarry tile floor, and the earth-toned walls blending with the mellow brickwork of the fireplace on the north wall.

I never allowed Eleanore to drive me anywhere again.

Her students and interns came and went. Even Dave eventually left the office to set up his own practice.

Eleanore died in 2003. Her obituary was long and impressive. I shed some tears, fondly remembering my eccentric friend and the beautifully designed houses she dreamed up.

THE CAT LADY OF INWOOD AVENUE

During the time we lived on Inwood Avenue (twenty-seven years), I became known as the cat lady of that street. Friends dropped off strays for reasons I never knew about, but it didn't matter much since they lived mostly outside. I even installed a cat door off the back porch.

Only two special cats, Wozzie and George, Don's favourites, were allowed to spend the night inside. Of all the cats, Wozzie was the most adventurous, often crossing busy Valley Road in search of new friends.

❧

Pets had been very much part of my childhood. I remembered the tame donkey and indoor cats at my grandfather's house in Wexford. As a city child, with my father's consulting rooms in our house on Fitzwilliam Place in Dublin, we were limited to small dogs. I loved our two playful Pekinese puppies, Socksie and Toto, with their bushy tails and protruding eyes, who slept on a doggy bed behind the secretary's office. Aunty Daisy and Daddy walked them around Fitzwilliam Square every evening before dinner, exchanging the news and gossip of the day. Mummy didn't mind animals so long as they didn't bark too much.

The only dogs Don knew were those on the family farm. When Margaret and John were very young, we bought Guinness, a pedigree yellow lab pup, who came with a cage where the children (mostly Margaret) liked to hide. Guinness grew up with the cats, who often curled up in a ball with him at the foot of the main staircase. Besides being a friendly creature, Guinness was the best substitute for a burglar alarm. At the sound of unfamiliar footsteps, his bark would scare the daylights out of the most astute burglar.

I was the dog walker. First thing before breakfast, Guinness and I did a few rounds of Anderson Park and headed out again during the day for more. Otherwise, our fenced-in back yard was available for him to play in. Don and Guinness were good friends, but he rarely had time to walk him. We enjoyed his presence for nine years.

We mourned our best friend and buried him under a dogwood tree in the back garden.

As a small boy, our son John had his own series of house pets, including gerbils, hamsters and snakes. Once, I found the snake he called Henry in his sock drawer.

Margaret also had her own pet, Tom, a black-and-white cat, who slept under the covers in her bed. The house was free of pets for a number of years, except for Wozzie and Don's cat, George, a sad-looking half-starved animal he had picked up on nearby Valley Road.

One day when I was working in real estate in a suburban neighbourhood of Newark, I saw a sad-looking dog on the side of the road – a beautiful mix of lab and Irish setter. I couldn't leave her there; she could barely stand. Timid at first, she struggled into the car, and we headed for the vet's office in Montclair. She had heartworm, among other ailments, and besides all that she had just had pups that were taken from her by another dog. The vet suggested I leave her there for a few days to recover. Don was furious.

"The last thing we need is another dog. Here you are working to make money for the children's college expenses, and now we have the extra cost of a vet!"

We had endless arguments until I brought the dog back from the vet. Charmed by her friendly nature and elegant appearance, he agreed we should keep her.

"Let's name her Cashel in memory of the happy times we had exploring the ruins," he said, referring to the burial place of Irish Kings dating back to the 4th and 5th Centuries. Brian Baru, the legendary high king of Ireland who drove out the Vikings, was buried there in 978.

Don produced a can of Guinness, and we toasted our new pet's health.

Cashel became part of our smaller family when the children went to college. The local kids loved to stroke her where she sat at the top of the front steps. Unlike Guinness, she didn't bark much and was happy to be left alone in the backyard. But she was terrified of other dogs, which forced me to walk her before 7am.

She continued to live with us until she came down with cancer shortly before we retired in 1995.

RETIREMENT TO WILMINGTON, NORTH CAROLINA

In the end, there were many reasons we ended up choosing Wilmington for our retirement.

As the most important historic city in the state of North Carolina, Wilmington offered all the cultural amenities we loved – music, art, and the theatre, as well as moderately priced housing and proximity to a beach. We were also within driving distance of Raleigh, the industrial triangle, UNC Chapel Hill, and a world-class medical centre at Duke University.

Wilmington, high on the banks of the Cape Fear River, would be our escape hatch from the cold northern winter.

❖·❖

Don loved to plan, so I left him to it and stayed behind cleaning up, selling most of the furniture and the house.

Joining him later in Wilmington, we stayed at an elegant B&B in the Historic District, with its wealth of 19th Century houses. There was an absence of Black people in the neighbourhood, and our hostess's smiles were a little too sugar coated, but I loved the idea of living in one of the small cottages behind the mansions. Don was totally against it.

"You may love historic buildings, but they can be cold and damp," he said. "Besides, I noticed an absence of Black people around the historic areas. We need to live in an integrated community."

Growing up in Europe, I knew little about the South except for the racial issues and a brief history of the Civil War I had found in my father's library. Many years later, in North Carolina, I found myself searching the history section of the Wilmington Public Library to learn more about it.

❖

When Don was in NYC on business, I checked with a realtor to look for some alternatives to the cottages in the Historic District that I had admired, but nothing clicked. There weren't any suburbs like the ones that existed in the larger northern cities. We needed to remember that North Carolina was a farming state, and we were looking for an integrated community close to the city.

I started to look at such places by myself and eventually found the perfect property on a dead-end street in Echo Farms. The two-acre lot played host to a modest Dutch Colonial house. It was about twenty minutes from the beach and a part of the Echo Farms organisation, a loosely bonded gated community with a nine-hole golf course and tennis courts. The view across the creek was spectacular. The porch smelled of pine needles and decay and needed to be enlarged, but we decided this could wait until we'd completed our move from New Jersey.

❧•❧

Although Echo Farms was an integrated community, we soon discovered, having read about the city's dark past, how the rules were different from those in New Jersey.

Despite some clumsy approaches, we became friends with the Black family living next door and found common interests. I played tennis with their daughter at the club and Don enjoyed chatting with her father.

Don became an active member of the Wilmington Garden Club, to the delight of our favourite neighbour Linda Snider, who was also a member, and though he wasn't the sporty type, he found he wasn't averse to a hike along marked trails. We made trips to Asheville in the mountains, after Margaret's in-laws moved there.

❧•❧

I applied for a job at the Historic Wilmington Foundation but it didn't work out, I suspect because of my age – mid-sixties. I did end up becoming an advisor and friend to the young woman who received the job, though.

I also volunteered at City Planning. The head of the Planning Board, Arcelia Wicker, a friendly and distinguished-looking Black man, eventually hired me as a consultant and later appointed me to write the Wilmington Design Guidelines for Historic Districts and Landmarks.

Don and I also joined the North Carolina Democrats and volunteered to help at the next election.

❧•❧

One day, an ad in the local paper caught my attention.

Agnes McDonald, retired professor of creative writing from UNC Wilmington offers courses in the Public Library. A delightful eccentric, direct and funny, Agnes lives in a small shed-like apartment with an assortment of smelly cats.

The group was small and diverse and exactly what I needed.

❧•❧

The years in Wilmington passed, and they were among the happiest times in our marriage. Retired life was full and rewarding. I volunteered at the new art museum, and Don advised retirees about their health insurance on a volunteer basis – he loved the work and appeared more relaxed than ever. We also took many trips to the beach in the evenings.

Relatives came from Europe and friends from New York.

When the writing group broke up, Agnes took me to the annual North Carolina Writers Conference.

I still remember the words of advice she offered me there: "Nothing is unpublishable, but always be truthful and make people laugh."

❧•❧

Impressed by its Spanish Baroque architecture, we joined St. Mary's Catholic Church in the Historic District, learning that it was the work of master builder Raphael Guastavino from Barcelona, Spain.[2] The church welcomed people in, no matter their denomination or colour.

---

[2] *Raphael Guastavino, a graduate master builder from the University of Barcelona, and his brother came to North Carolina in 1881 to introduce the Catalan Vault, allowing for large, uncluttered spaces. Grand Central Station, the New York Museum of Science, and the Church of St. John the Divine are just a few of the buildings where patents were placed. St. Mary's Church in Wilmington and the Basilica of Saint Lawrence in Ashville, now listed as shrines, could have been the first to receive patents. They are also listed on the National Register of Historic Places.*

DON'S FINAL ILLNESS AND DEATH

One day after a long walk on the beach, Don complained of chest pains and exhaustion. His local cardiologist revealed that two of his arteries were blocked.

But Don said that he needed another opinion, so we flew to NYC, where we stayed with friends so he could visit his regular heart specialist, who diagnosed he had non-Hodgkin's lymphoma.

"Yes, there are treatments, but they are still at the experimental stage," the doctor said. "You can rest at home for a while, but eventually you should go to the hospital."

❧•❧

I knew his days were numbered. We decided to return to Wilmington. Don, ever hopeful, contacted his friend Jim Levitan, whose son-in-law was the head of the Cleveland Clinic. We even flew out to see him.

The news was much the same as we had heard in NYC. Don had stage 4 cancer, and there was no more to be said.

❧•❧

Don was stalwart and accepted his fate. He remained cheery. Over the summer, old friends came to visit; friends and neighbours dropped by with food. Our large screened-in back porch became the living room.

He would say, "I've had a wonderful life – a loving wife, two children, two grandchildren, and many friends. What more can you expect!"

I called the children. Margaret and her husband Cador Pricejones were now living in Somerville, Massachusetts. John was out of the country.

The children were scheduled to arrive before Thanksgiving. I had a premonition that Don would die over the weekend and e-mailed his sister Lorraine in Minnesota, as well as my family in Ireland and the UK.

That weekend, Don was rested and composed. Local friends, David and Cathy Hume and Hilda Godwin, dropped by. Our favourite neighbour, Linda Snider, helped with food supplies.

All was well through the fall. We still went out to his favourite restaurants and watched movies on TV.

❧•❧

A few weeks before Thanksgiving, Don almost collapsed, and we went to the hospital. He had a nice room on the oncology ward, a cheerful place with brightly coloured walls, and hanging plants. I met the nursing staff, a cheerful group – both male and female. When he was settled in, I was urged to leave.

Outside, a leaden sky suggested rain. Thunder growled in the distance, and the moist air relaxed my tired body. I ran for the car as lightning flashed across the sky.

The rain came down in torrents. I entered the silent house and called the cats. They were scared stiff, hiding under the living room sofa and refusing to budge. The loblolly pines swished back and forth in a frenzied dance as the creek water rose. Sleep came slowly. Don's now favourite cat, Rebecca, was slow to settle down and kept to Don's side of our large bed.

❧•❧

Some years prior, Don had bought a plot in the original section of the Oakdale Cemetery. It was advertised for sale in the local paper and had become a big joke between us, since I had given tours of the cemetery and told him of the quirky characters buried there.

"When I join their ranks, I wonder what the next guide will say about me?" Don would laugh.

He had several requests in the lead up to his passing – he wanted there to be no public viewing at the funeral, and he didn't want to use a ventilator to take his last breath.

Don left me the phone number of monks in Wisconsin who made simple pine caskets. I knew this would upset the undertakers, but I didn't care; they had plenty of business.

❧•❧

I paid daily visits to the hospital during the week before Thanksgiving. What kept him going were jokes about lawyers told by an amusing male nurse, who was a retired lawyer himself. His favourite priest from St. Mary's gave him communion.

When the children arrived two days before the holiday, Don made a big effort to dress in his favourite robe. I stayed with him all night at the hospital; he was restless and out of it most of the time. I refused the offer of a ventilator.

By then, I was starting to fall apart and was scared of fainting. When Don settled down towards dawn, the nurse suggested I go home. She said she would phone me if the situation worsened. I drove home and collapsed into bed, only learning the next morning that he had died during the night.

Of course, I felt guilty, but there was no going back.

❧•❧

Margaret and Cador took care of the toddlers, Esmay and Powell, and I put my emotions on hold. The tears could come later; there was too much to be done.

I emailed my family in Ireland and the UK, as well as Don's sister in Minnesota. Holding the funeral after ten days allowed time for us to get the pine box from Wisconsin and work with the local funeral home as to how we could handle it.

We needed clothes for the funeral and went shopping in the morning. The men all had dark school blazers, Margaret picked up a beautiful dark-blue silk dress, and I found a much-needed black suit at Talbots. In the afternoon, I tackled the task of writing Don's obituary for the local paper.

In place of a viewing, family members and friends gathered for a wine and cheese reception in one of the church halls, sharing their personal stories about Don. It was the modern version of an Irish wake.

A nun from St. Ann's Church helped me with Don's favourite hymns. Everything went according to plan. The children gave brief eulogies of their father, and the hymns were beautiful.

After a simple burial service at Oakdale Cemetery, we adjourned to our house in Echo Farms for a gathering of the clans – just the way he'd wanted it!

❖

I'm alone now with grief and so many tears.

Our dream house in Wilmington, North Carolina.

MARY ROSE HOGAN

An impending snowstorm forced me home early one day. It was late February in Harvard Square and bitterly cold. I shivered and shook snowflakes from my coat. The phone rang. The ringing came from my landline, which was reserved for family calls. These usually only came on the weekend.

I answered the phone to a clipped English voice; it was my nephew, Chris Hogan.

"Hi, Eleanor. I'm afraid it's bad news. Mum had a severe stroke this morning. The doctors think she's unlikely to recover."

My stomach dropped. I tried to steady myself and remain calm. I wondered to myself how I could help while over in America. "Who can I phone?"

"I've been in touch with the English and Irish family," he continued calmly. "Alice and I are both in Bath staying with Dad. We'll keep you posted."

❖

Mary Rose was the most agreeable of my sisters, and the most like Mummy in appearance and manner, though she lacked my mother's ability to act helpless and get her own way. Generous to a fault, she was always ready to help. She was pretty, soft-spoken, and conservative. We would discuss books and world events, but rarely spoke of politics and religion. Suddenly, without her, I felt desolate and alone.

I couldn't believe it. Mary Rose and I had spoken on the phone just two days ago. I could still hear her voice.

"The holidays were wonderful. Chris rented a house in the neighbourhood, and all the grandchildren came. They cooked Christmas dinner, and we were their guests!" she had said.

I was confused and angry. The cats were rubbing my feet, and their fur was comforting. I felt the need to talk and share my anxieties, so I called my daughter Margaret in nearby Somerville. She and her husband Cador had visited Bath with their children five years ago. She was the only one near me who could understand.

❖

The week loomed ahead with a tight schedule of classes and local obligations. I made myself a cup of strong tea, fed the cat, and tried to make sense of what had happened to my sister.

Everything went wrong after she broke her hip. She had never completed rehab and still had difficulty walking. On my last visit a year prior, I had taken her for walks along the canal behind her house. Her husband Barry wasn't much help and never encouraged her in the long recovery.

There were no changes over the weekend. My youngest sister Esmay, who lived in Dublin, happened to be in London visiting her daughter Jessica during this time, so she had gone to Bath to be with the Hogans. She reported the news to me.

"She looked so peaceful when we went to the hospital this morning," she told me. "Barry is bearing up well. Don't call. I'll keep you posted."

⋘•⋙

Mary Rose died the following Tuesday. Chris delivered the message in a calm, deliberate way, his emotions kept tightly under control.

"She just stopped breathing. It was quiet and peaceful. I hope you can come to the funeral."

My anger faded. I tried to sound sympathetic and calm, assuring him that, of course, I would come to the funeral.

After the call ended, I proceeded to look for the earliest flight to London. Margaret agreed to come with me to the funeral. She liked Mary Rose and knew I needed her emotional support.

We arrived in Heathrow the following day, where Barbara, Chris' wife, had organised a car and driver for our trip to Wimbledon, where they lived. Their house on Dora Road had long been a second home for me on my many visits to the UK before and after Don died.

Chris had just returned from Bath and would drive us back there the next day.

***

It was bitterly cold on the motorway. Freezing rain lashed against the car windows. A few hours after our dreary and uneventful journey, we reached Barry's house, a faceless semi-detached villa, part of a development built in the shadow of the historic Georgian mansions along the London Road. The area was known as Lark Hall.

Barry and Mary Rose had retired to Bath about twenty years ago. My sister loved her adopted country, especially Bath, where she became part of the community, volunteering at historic sites and helping out at the local church. She had become more English than the English themselves, much to the amusement of her Irish relatives. But no one in the family really minded, knowing she was happy and well.

Her daughter Alice, a tall handsome redhead, was busy sorting food and organising sleeping arrangements with the help of her unmarried brother John. Alice welcomed us with hugs and cups of hot tea.

"I'm trying to organise lesson plans between the funeral stuff – but thank you for coming. I know Dad is delighted," she said. Alice was an elementary school teacher with three children. She glanced wistfully at her father.

Barry was sprawled on the sofa, his face white and empty. I was shocked by his appearance, so different from his usual straight-backed military presence.

"I can't believe she's gone," he murmured hoarsely. "What can I do? I can't be without her!"

I took his hand and kissed it gently, something I would never have done in the past. I tried to distract him – asking about his childhood in Burma and his days at boarding school, but to no avail. He was in another world.

"We had to move his bed downstairs into the dining room since Mum's death," said Alice. "John and I will stay with him here. You and Margaret should meet the Irish relatives downtown."

⬥⬥⬥

I was so glad to see John Hogan. As Mary Rose's middle child, he was different from his siblings. An artist and lover of the outdoors, he was more at home as a naturalist and painter than sitting at an office desk.

Mary Rose had encouraged him to exhibit his paintings at local art shows and worried about his future. She'd found him a flat in one of the historic buildings nearby. Tall, attractive, and shy, he resembled his mother more than his siblings. They had been very close. He had remained nearby, working as a gardener and landscape assistant at a large private school in the neighbourhood.

After chatting with John, Margaret and I took a cab to a quiet pub near the Crescent. It was bitterly cold and almost dark when we left Lark Hall for the gathering. We found Caroline Twiss (my sister Ann's daughter) and her husband Eoghan, my sister Esmay, and her daughter Katy all sitting in a corner. Caroline hugged us with tears in her eyes.

"We are here for the family, Mum decided not to come – her husband Dick has the flu."

Caroline, Eoghan, and their children were close to Chris and Barbara. The two couples took trips to Europe, and the Hogans had visited the Twiss farm in Portlaoise.

My youngest sister Esmay looked angry. "I can't believe it. Chris told me this morning that Barry, unbeknown to the family, made arrangements some time ago for Mary Rose to be cremated."

I agreed with Esmay, knowing that my conservative Catholic sister would have liked a traditional burial, but this was not the time for family wars. Margaret and I left early, still jet lagged and eager to sleep.

❧•❧

The weather cleared and sunbeams danced across the altar of the old church on the day of the funeral. Chris had to hire a wheelchair and a large taxi to take Barry from Lark Hall to the church. Barry and Chris arrived early.

I was distracted, looking for old friends and relatives who had started to fill the pews. Chris gave a wonderful tribute to his mother. His daughter Veronica recited a poem, and her brother Louis added a personal story of his granny.

After the service, Esmay and I attended the reception feeling sad that she was cremated. On reflection, I recognise it was probably the right thing to do, considering how far apart some of us lived.

❧•❧

For me, this was the end of an era. I'd had a love affair with Bath ever since the Hogans had retired there. Visiting the museum on the Crescent, where Mary Rose had worked, or the Abbey, where Barry gave guided tours, had become rituals for me.

Even just meandering through the narrow streets of Bath filled me with dreams of Jane Austen, Beau Nash, and other pleasure seekers of their time. Otherwise, it was afternoon tea at the assembly rooms, or a visit to the Roman Spa, now modernised with the addition of a heated swimming pool on the roof.

It occurred to me that this could be my last visit to this elegant Georgian city with its Crescent, squares and colourful past.

❧✿☙

Barry's health fell apart. Chris stayed with him in Bath for a while; John and other family members visited. Sadly, he never recovered and died six months later.

THE CELTIC TIGER, AND
A CHANGING CITY

The Celtic Tiger refers to the economy of the Republic of Ireland from the mid-1990s to the late 2000s, a period of vast economic growth funded by direct foreign investors.

The Conservative party averaged 9.4% growth through the 2000s. The demographics of the country and the increased number of women in the workforce contributed to this unusual growth.

❧❦

The plane seemed colder than usual. *Maybe it's lack of sleep?*

My feet were freezing. I dozed fitfully as I always did on these trips. My body complained. I should have remembered that everything outside North Carolina seemed cold.

After a few minutes, the lights came on. I smelled coffee and could hear the rustling of trays. Soon, I'd be forced to eat. The woman beside me was moving around.

She'd wanted to chat, mostly about her lost make-up and a hiking trip she would take in Cork, where her husband had a consulting job. I'd learned that her name was Laura, and that she worked with an insurance company in Philadelphia. The job was tough and intense – she needed exercise and fresh air. I assured her she'd get plenty of that in Cork, remembering a camping trip from my student days, when it had rained so much that my father had had to rescue us from our water-laden tent. It seemed trivial, but I was glad to listen. I'd been self-preoccupied for too long and needed to communicate. But now it was early morning, and I wasn't keen on conversation.

❧•❧

It had always been like this on flights, especially the long ones. I enjoyed the feeling of being suspended and free as the clouds scudding across the sky. I'd flown across the Atlantic so many times, but this trip was different. I was travelling alone and more anxious than I liked to admit. Don never talked much on our trips together, but he took care of the details and was a strong presence.

It had been difficult to get away. I was tired and worried about leaving the house, the cats, and the garden. Ordinary things became stressful. I needed to go, not in the sense of running away, but rather to be with the familiar, only in a different place.

I was taking a trip to Ireland, one that Don and I had planned the year before he died.

❧•❧

Some passengers were standing now, others still huddling in blankets. There was already a long line for the rest room. I decided to wait. The flight attendant was handing out papers for immigration. Streaks of sunshine played on the cabin walls, making me feel much warmer. The coffee smelled good but tasted like dishwater. Maybe it was the Styrofoam cups.

Laura turned around and smiled. Her teeth seemed too small for her large mouth. She had hazel eyes and white alabaster skin, the sort that always looked good. *Why is she fussing so much about her lost make up?* I wondered. I was feeling scruffy and searched for a lipstick. *We should be on the ground soon, and I will find something else to worry about, like finding my sister in the crowded airport.*

The landing was bumpy. After disembarking, we walked through endless corridors, up and down escalators, to the immigration hall, a well organised group of tired, silent people. It was more efficient and business-like than I remembered. Clear-skinned Irish faces waved us through. I walked briskly towards the barrier, searching for my sister Esmay.

It wasn't long before I saw her, smiling and waving in front of the barrier. Her bouncy hair was fashionably cut, skin lightly tanned, and she was wearing yellow jeans. We shared a brief hug before she grabbed my single case, and we headed for the parking lot. The air was cool, damp, and refreshing, a 'soft day' in the local jargon.

"I love your jacket," Esmay remarked as we searched for the car. I likewise commented on her new hairstyle, remembering how direct sisters could be.

While she drove us away from the airport, I waited for her to comment on my additional wrinkles and lack of make-up, but she was too focused on finding the on-ramp for the highway. I was pleased she had remarked on my jacket, which was unusual and made from brightly coloured quilted cotton. It occurred to me then that I might have bought it to impress her rather than please myself. We were surprisingly alike, despite the large age gap between us – both outgoing and competitive – which made for a strong relationship.

Traffic inched along the four-lane highway towards the city. Visibility was poor, though it wasn't raining. Seeing the road signs in kilometres reminded me that Ireland was now part of the EU.

"It will take forever to get through the city," said Esmay drily. "I only meet family who come from overseas these days, everyone else takes the bus."

It happened to be rush hour when we were travelling. *What can you expect?* I thought wryly to myself. A thriving economy meant more traffic, congestion, and impatient drivers.

I missed the old highway, banked with daffodils in the spring and strewn with leaves in autumn. Maybe it took more time, but now all we had was more traffic and high baffles to reduce the noise.

As we drove, I could see outlines of the city through the morning mist. Building cranes like giant robots dotted the skyline, and new high-rise buildings mingled with the old familiar ones. At the centre of O' Connell Street, a stainless-steel monument called the Spike had replaced the classical pillar from which Lord Nelson had surveyed the city, until the IRA decided to blow him to pieces in 1966.

"It's supposed to be a symbol of modern Ireland," said Esmay. "Critics were vicious at first, but it's becoming more accepted. It also forces the city to landscape the street."

I was sorry to see Lord Nelson go, despite his association with colonial rule. It was a handsome statue and a familiar landmark. I wasn't too sure about the Spike.

I became lost in thoughts of the Dublin of my youth. I didn't know much about O'Connell Street until I was about twelve years old. In those days, everything north of the Liffey was considered overcrowded and full of pickpockets and undesirables – not a place for small children to explore. It was a long way from Fitzwilliam Place, and my snobbish mother, who didn't drive, would have had no reason to go there. Aunty Daisy would occasionally talk about the antique shops, the book dealers on the quays in front of the Four Courts, and the outdoor markets on Moore Street, but we never went there until we were older.

"You must look at the new buildings in the financial centre behind the Custom House," said my sister, interrupting my reverie and pointing to a silhouette of glass and steel etched against the sky.

I was more interested in the classical Custom House and reminded her that I was part of a team that measured the building during my first year at architectural school.

"I was just a little girl then," said Esmay, smiling, "and not the least bit interested in what you were up to. So, what happened?"

I told her that, for me, it had been a fiasco. With just three girls in the program, the boys tried to take over everything. Either to show off, or just to prove we were tough, the girls agreed to work on the roof, which, though protected by a stone balustrade, was very high above the street. Scared to admit my fear of heights, I quickly became dizzy and felt like throwing up. The professor, Mattie McDermot, who disliked having women in the program, accused me of wasting time. I was relegated to measuring windows on the street level, which the other students thought to be a huge joke. Apart from a loss of dignity, I survived the incident and most of my measurements added up.

As I spoke, we crossed Butt Bridge and headed down the quays towards the port, a grey industrial area between the Custom House and the Poolbeg Generating Station at the mouth of the river. I remembered the stone buildings being blackened from the coal-burning factories and the plants that spewed endless smoke across the sky. Stevedores and vagrants had lived in the small brick row houses along the river for generations. You could buy fish at the markets along the quays and smell the yeast from Boland's Bread Company. Though colourful by day, it had a reputation for the overwhelming number of street brawls and the pickpockets who came out at night; it was not a place to wander after dark.

"It's become a fashionable section to live in these days. The small houses are sought after by young professionals who want to be close to their work," said Esmay.

Now it was almost too clean, and the smells had gone. I observed the glass-fronted apartment buildings occupying empty lots, the stone warehouses that had been turned into office spaces, and the flowering trees along the waterfront. As we passed the tollbooth and turned south towards Ringsend, I wondered about the dock workers that were displaced. Had they moved to another part of the city or just fled to the outer suburbs?

A spray of salt air swept through the open car window, and a flight of sea gulls swooped down from nowhere. We finally reached Sandymount Strand, heading south along the coast road to Dún Laoghaire. It always seemed like low tide at Sandymount, a flat expanse of sand that was too shallow for swimming but wonderful for jogging, horse riding, or just sitting on the sea wall and watching the sun rise above Howth Head.

It was much the same as I remembered – the familiar sea wall and the stucco-faced unpretentious houses sitting primly on their separate lots behind cast-iron fences. The squat Martello Tower seemed timeless and familiar, its granite walls sparkling in the morning sun.

"The Tower is now an upscale restaurant," said Esmay.

The Tower was one of seventy four structures built along the coast in 1810 by the British Admiralty during the Napoleonic Wars. Powder guns were mounted on the roof, and a shot furnace that could heat the cannon balls was built into the parapet. The dubious effectiveness of the structures was never contested. Over time, many fell into disuse, others were turned into residences and restaurants. One in Sandycove, a suburb further along the coast, had been rented to Oliver St. John Gogarty and

James Joyce in 1904 and was now a museum commemorating the works of Joyce.

"I still swim at the Forty Foot," said Esmay, referring to the rocky swimming area behind Joyce's tower. "You must remember when only men were allowed to swim there. Now that it's unisex, we have to wear swimsuits."

❧•❧

After a little while, we returned to the main road, already full of commuter traffic heading towards the city. In the summer during World War II, we would sometimes take the #10 tram along the same route. It took forever, but we didn't care, it was fun just to sit on the upper deck, snoop at the gardens along the way, and look forward to a swim at the Dún Laoghaire Baths or off the rocks at Sandycove.

"I have vague memories of the trams," said Esmay, "though I do remember the bus. We had moved from Fitzwilliam Place by the time I was allowed to go swimming without supervision, and by that time, cars were back on the road and Aunty Daisy would sometimes let me drive hers."

In recent years, a rapid transit system known as the Dart had replaced both the tram and the bus.

"It relieves the congestion and saves petrol. I rarely take the car into town now," said Esmay.

As a supporter of rapid transit for larger cities, I didn't really miss the lumbering tram or the bus that stopped at almost every corner.

We passed Monkstown, with its trees and parks alongside its elegant, terraced houses, high above the road, now painted in various pastel colours. Many landmarks had disappeared. The Salthill Hotel, a flamboyant Victorian structure, where my parents had a reception after their wedding in a nearby church, had become a faceless office block.

As we headed along the coast towards Sandycove, where Esmay and her family lived, she talked about selling her family house.

"Katy is planning her wedding for next year. Eva and Jessie have their own places, and William has a flat in Killiney. Now is the perfect time to sell," she said. "But Michael won't even talk about it. You know how he loves to entertain."

We finally arrived at Corrigmore, one of the many villas built in Edwardian times when middle-class families left the dirt and squalor of the city for fresh air and a more salubrious lifestyle.

Though Mummy had died in its front drawing room, I had good memories of the house; my niece Eva had her wedding reception in the walled garden, and my own children had romped and picked daisies on the grass during their Irish vacations.

❖

Michael Rothschild, Esmay's husband, greeted us warmly with the promise of a good lunch. A large amusing man, he was a former rugby player, the son of a Holocaust survivor and an Irish mother. Michael was proud of his Jewish heritage and one of the most religious members of the family. Now retired from the business world, he was working on a BA at University College Dublin, as well as sailing, cooking, and visiting his many family members. On top of all that, he still managed to be entertaining and funny.

After lunch and a nap, Esmay and I walked up Killiney Hill. The mist cleared as we reached the top, streaks of sunlight broke through the tangled undergrowth as we scrambled up the steep path. Quincy, Esmay's elderly Jack Russell, could barely make it to the summit. The view of Dublin Bay in one direction and the coastline to Bray Head in the other was as spectacular as ever.

Don, a midwestern product of the Land of Lakes, had loved this view of the ocean, though he was amused by an obelisk honouring Queen Victoria.

I felt peace there, a sense of home and belonging. My world was tranquil, at least for a while.

❦

The post-2008 Irish downturn corresponded with a series of banking scandals. Emigration out of the country escalated rapidly, more to Australia and New Zealand than to the United States. Ireland was the first state in the Eurozone to enter recession. Today, the country has a thriving economy. It is sixth on the index of economic freedom and ranks first for high-value direct investment.

THE REST OF THE STORY

After Don was diagnosed with cancer in early 2004, and until his death later that year, writing kept me sane. I lingered in Wilmington for the year after his death sorting out my emotions, finances and papers.

Would I sell my house with its flowers, birds and wooded creek and move to a condo in downtown Wilmington? Perhaps I would go back to the north with its long winters and crowds?

As I contemplated the move, a phone call from my daughter Margaret in Somerville, Massachusetts, gave me another option. She invited me to move to the Boston area, which gave me the opportunity to help with her three year old twins, Esmay and Powell. I disliked snow and wasn't looking forward to the harsh weather, but my future was decided.

I put my house in Echo Farms on the market, had a porch sale, and contacted a mover. Before the actual move, I flew north and, with the help of my son-in-law Cador Pricejones, found a delightful apartment on Lee Street in Cambridge, not far from Somerville.

A few weeks later, I said a reluctant goodbye to my friends and set off with my two cats, Rachael and Rebecca, on the long trip to New England. Fortunately, a dear friend, June Davison, came along to share the driving.

I quickly settled into the Lee Street apartment, with its open porches and honeysuckle hedge along the garage driveway. Once a week I picked up Esmay and Powell from their Somerville playschool. After lunch and a nap, we explored the neighbourhood playgrounds, made card-houses on the dining room table, read stories, and learned how to cook. Powell's favourite was a recipe for pumpkin bread from the *Crane House Cookbook* I had used in Montclair, New Jersey. Esmay enjoyed my cats Rachel and Rebecca. On overnight visits, the twins liked to cuddle up in my bed, which left me with many cherished memories.

I joined the local Y and met friends in the neighbourhood. I felt welcomed at St. Paul's Church in Cambridge, and heard about HILR, the Harvard Institute for Learning in Retirement, from Stacy Carmichael, a friend from Montclair now living in Cambridge. I was fortunate enough to be accepted and am still there thirteen years later.

New doors opened and friendships flourished. I listened to the Boston Symphony, explored the art museums, and learnt how to travel alone on group tours to Russia, Sicily, and the Middle East – even to Egypt during the Arab Spring. But I never went back to the countries I had visited with Don.

❦

A few years later, I needed to look for a new apartment because of construction on the Lee Street house. Having lived mostly in historic houses, I now wanted something new and different.

I found just that on Harvey Street in North Cambridge, where a former ice-cream factory had been converted into apartments. Since one was available, I paid a month's rent and moved right in. The cats and I thrived in our new home with its sunlit spaces and amazing views.

Even now, memories of early dawn and sunsets over the bike path from my balcony bed float through my dreams.

⚡

But again, change was inevitable. The landlord was slow to fix everything, including the sidewalks and driveway. Getting in and out of the basement parking garage became a nightmare. When I fell and almost broke my nose, and my feisty cat Rebecca died, I knew it was time to move.

Once again, fortune smiled. My son-in-law, Cador, was thinking of updating the first-floor apartment of their two-family house in Somerville. It became a joint venture. Cador and I worked out the spaces. My now teenaged grandkids, worked over the winter months and I moved into Sycamore Street in early March, exhausted but grateful to those who made it possible.

⚡

When COVID-19 hit on March 20, 2020, our extended family became our bubble, sharing company and eating dinner together. My grandkids entertained friends on the front porch and were only allowed inside the house after a negative test.

We were lucky, and nobody except Cador got sick – and it was a mild case. The grandchildren discovered the joy of cooking. Powell made amazing sandwiches, and Esmay baked biscuits and cakes.

I enjoyed zoom classes at HILR, and scaling the steep hills of Somerville for peace and fresh air. When the pandemic receded, I flew across the Atlantic to see family and friends.

❈

Now, the kids are at college, and my daughter is at work. Life seems normal and free. But the planet's in trouble with earthquakes and floods.

❈

Just tighten your seat belts and wait for the bump.

Rachael and Rebecca.

ABOUT THE AUTHOR

Eleanor McArevey was born in Dublin, Ireland, and grew up during World War II. She has a degree in Architecture from University College Dublin. Eleanor worked briefly in Southern Rhodesia, now Zimbabwe, and later emigrated to the United States, where she married Don Price, a lawyer from Minnesota, and lived in Montclair, New Jersey. She received a Master of Science in Historic Preservation from Columbia University. While living in Wilmington, North Carolina, Eleanor took a creative writing course and launched her passion for the creative word. She continued her education with courses at the Harvard Institute for Learning in Retirement. She joined a writing group and continues to write today.